Veloce *Classic Reprint* Series

Karmann Ghia
Coupé & Cabriolet

Malcolm Bobbitt

VELOCE PUBLISHING
THE PUBLISHER OF FINE AUTOMOTIVE BOOKS

Also from Veloce Publishing:

SpeedPro Series
Aerodynamics of Your Road Car, Modifying the (Edgar and Barnard)
Camshafts – How to Choose & Time Them For Maximum Power (Hammill)
Custom Air Suspension – How to install air suspension in your road car – on a budget! (Edgar)
Cylinder Heads, How to Build, Modify & Power Tune – Updated & Revised Edition (Burgess & Gollan)
Distributor-type Ignition Systems, How to Build & Power Tune – New 3rd Edition (Hammill)
Ford SOHC 'Pinto' & Sierra Cosworth DOHC Engines, How to Power Tune – Updated & Enlarged Edition (Hammill)
Ford V8, How to Power Tune Small Block Engines (Hammill)
Holley Carburetors, How to Build & Power Tune – Revised & Updated Edition (Hammill)
Retro or classic car for high performance, How to modify your (Stapleton)
Secrets of Speed – Today's techniques for 4-stroke engine blueprinting & tuning (Swager)
V8 Engine, How to Build a Short Block For High Performance (Hammill)
Weber DCOE, & Dellorto DHLA Carburetors, How to Build & Power Tune – 3rd Edition (Hammill)

Workshop Pro Series
Setting up a home car workshop (Edgar)
Car electrical and electronic systems (Edgar)

Enthusiast's Restoration Manual Series
Classic Car Bodywork, How to Restore (Thaddeus)
Classic Car Electrics (Thaddeus)
Classic Cars, How to Paint (Thaddeus)
How to Restore & Improve Classic Car Suspension, Steering & Wheels (Parish – translator)

Essential Buyer's Guide Series
Ford Capri (Paxton)
Ford Escort Mk1 & Mk2 (Williamson)
Ford Model A – All Models 1927 to 1931 (Buckley)
Ford Model T – All models 1909 to 1927 (Barker)
Ford Mustang – First Generation 1964 to 1973 (Cook)
Ford Mustang (Cook)
Ford RS Cosworth Sierra & Escort (Williamson)

Those Were The Days ... Series
American 'Independent' Automakers – AMC to Willys 1945 to 1960 (Mort)
American Station Wagons – The Golden Era 1950-1975 (Mort)
American Trucks of the 1950s (Mort)
American Trucks of the 1960s (Mort)
American Woodies 1928-1953 (Mort)
Anglo-American Cars from the 1930s to the 1970s (Mort)

General
1½-litre GP Racing 1961-1965 (Whitelock)
Alfa Tipo 33 (McDonough & Collins)
Alpine & Renault – The Development of the Revolutionary Turbo F1 Car 1968 to 1979 (Smith)
Alpine & Renault – The Sports Prototypes 1963 to 1969 (Smith)
Alpine & Renault – The Sports Prototypes 1973 to 1978 (Smith)
Bahamas Speed Weeks, The (O'Neil)
BMW 5-Series (Cranswick)
BMW Z-Cars (Taylor)
BMW Classic 5 Series 1972 to 2003 (Cranswick)
BMW – The Power of M (Vivian)
British at Indianapolis, The (Wagstaff)
BRM – A Mechanic's Tale (Salmon)
BRM V16 (Ludvigsen)
Carrera Panamericana, La (Tipler)
Chrysler 300 – America's Most Powerful Car 2nd Edition (Ackerson)
Chrysler PT Cruiser (Ackerson)
Citroën DS (Bobbitt)
Cobra – The Real Thing! (Legate)
Competition Car Aerodynamics 3rd Edition (McBeath)
Competition Car Composites A Practical Handbook (Revised 2nd Edition) (McBeath)
Cortina – Ford's Bestseller (Robson)
Cosworth – The Search for Power (6th edition) (Robson)
Daily Mirror 1970 World Cup Rally 40, The (Robson)
Daimler SP250 New Edition (Long)
Datsun Fairlady Roadster to 280ZX – The Z-Car Story (Long)
Dino – The V6 Ferrari (Long)
Dodge Challenger & Plymouth Barracuda (Grist)
Dodge Charger – Enduring Thunder (Ackerson)
Dodge Dynamite! (Grist)
Fast Ladies – Female Racing Drivers 1888 to 1970 (Bouzanquet)
Fate of the Sleeping Beauties, The (op de Weegh/Hottendorff/op de Weegh)
Ferrari 288 GTO, The Book of the (Sackey)
Ferrari 333 SP (O'Neil)
Fiat & Abarth 124 Spider & Coupé (Tipler)
Fiat & Abarth 500 & 600 – 2nd Edition (Bobbitt)
Fiats, Great Small (Ward)
Ford Cleveland 335-Series V8 engine 1970 to 1982 – The Essential Source Book (Hammill)
Ford F100/F150 Pick-up 1948-1996 (Ackerson)
Ford F150 Pick-up 1997-2005 (Ackerson)
Ford Focus WRC (Robson)
Ford GT – Then, and Now (Streather)
Ford GT40 (Legate)
Ford Midsize Muscle – Fairlane, Torino & Ranchero (Cranswick)
Ford Model Y (Roberts)
Ford Small Block V8 Racing Engines 1962-1970 – The Essential Source Book (Hammill)
Ford Thunderbird From 1954, The Book of the (Long)
Formula One – The Real Score? (Harvey)
Formula 5000 Motor Racing, Back then ... and back now (Lawson)
Forza Minardi! (Vigar)
Grand Prix Ferrari – The Years of Enzo Ferrari's Power, 1948-1980 (Pritchard)
Grand Prix Ford – DFV-powered Formula 1 Cars (Robson)
GT – The World's Best GT Cars 1953-73 (Dawson)
Hillclimbing & Sprinting – The Essential Manual (Short & Wilkinson)
Honda NSX
How to Restore & Improve Classic Car Suspension, Steering & Wheels (Parish, translator)
Intermeccanica – The Story of the Prancing Bull (McCredie & Reisner)
Jaguar from the shop floor (Martin)
Jaguar E-type Factory and Private Competition Cars (Griffiths)
Jaguar, The Rise of (Price)
Jaguar XJ 220 – The Inside Story (Moreton)
Jaguar XJ-S, The Book of the (Long)
Jeep CJ (Ackerson)
Jeep Wrangler (Ackerson)
Karmann-Ghia Coupé & Convertible (Bobbitt)
Lamborghini Miura Bible, The (Sackey)
Lamborghini Murciélago, The book of the (Pathmanathan)
Lamborghini Urraco, The Book of the (Landsem)
Lambretta Bible, The (Davies)
Lancia 037 (Collins)
Lancia Delta HF Integrale (Blaettel & Wagner)
Lancia Delta Integrale (Collins)
Le Mans Panoramic (Ireland)
Lexus Story, The (Long)
Lola – The Illustrated History (1957-1977) (Starkey)
Lola – All the Sports Racing & Single-seater Racing Cars 1978-1997 (Starkey)
Lola T70 – The Racing History & Individual Chassis Record – 4th Edition (Starkey)
Lotus 18 Colin Chapman's U-turn (Whitelock)
Lotus 49 (Oliver)
Maserati 250F In Focus (Pritchard)
Mazda MX-5/Miata 1.6 Enthusiast's Workshop Manual (Grainger & Shoemark)
Mazda MX-5/Miata 1.8 Enthusiast's Workshop Manual (Grainger & Shoemark)
Mazda MX-5 Miata, The book of the – The 'Mk1' NA-series 1988 to 1997 (Long)
Mazda MX-5 Miata, The book of the – The 'Mk2' NB-series 1997 to 2004 (Long)
Mazda MX-5 Miata Roadster (Long)
Mazda Rotary-engined Cars (Cranswick)
Mercedes-Benz SL – R230 series 2001 to 2011 (Long)
Mercedes-Benz SL – W113 series 1963-1971 (Long)
Mercedes-Benz SL & SLC – 107-series 1971-1989 (Long)
Mercedes-Benz SLK – R170 series 1996-2004 (Long)
Mercedes-Benz SLK – R171 series 2004-2011 (Long)
Mercedes-Benz W123-series – All models 1976 to 1986 (Long)
Mercedes G-Wagen (Long)
Micro Trucks (Mort)
Mitsubishi Lancer Evo, The Road Car & WRC Story (Long)
Montlhéry, The Story of the Paris Autodrome (Boddy)
MOPAR Muscle – Barracuda, Dart & Valiant 1960-1980 (Cranswick)
Motor Racing – Reflections of a Lost Era (Carter)
Motor Racing – The Pursuit of Victory 1930-1962 (Carter)
Motor Racing – The Pursuit of Victory 1963-1972 (Wyatt/Sears)
Motor Racing Heroes – The Stories of 100 Greats (Newman)
Motorsport In colour, 1950s (Wainwright)
N.A.R.T. – A concise history of the North American Racing Team 1957 to 1983 (O'Neil)
Nissan 300ZX & 350Z – The Z-Car Story (Long)
Nissan GT-R Supercar: Born to race (Gorodji)
Northeast American Sports Car Races 1950-1959 (O'Neil)
Pontiac Firebird – New 3rd Edition (Cranswick)
Porsche 356 (2nd Edition) (Long)
Porsche 908 (Födisch, Neßhöver, Roßbach, Schwarz & Roßbach)
Porsche 911 Carrera – The Last of the Evolution (Corlett)
Porsche 911R, RS & RSR, 4th Edition (Starkey)
Porsche 911, The Book of the (Long)
Porsche 911 – The Definitive History 2004-2012 (Long)
Porsche – The Racing 914s (Smith)
Porsche 911SC 'Super Carrera' – The Essential Companion (Streather)
Porsche 914 & 914-6: The Definitive History of the Road & Competition Cars (Long)
Porsche 924 (Long)
The Porsche 924 Carreras – evolution to excellence (Smith)
Porsche 928 (Long)
Porsche 930 to 935: The Turbo Porsches (Starkey)
Porsche 944 (Long)
Porsche 964, 993 & 996 Data Plate Code Breaker (Streather)
Porsche 993 'King Of Porsche' – The Essential Companion (Streather)
Porsche 996 'Supreme Porsche' – The Essential Companion (Streather)
Porsche 997 2004-2012 – Porsche Excellence (Streather)
Porsche Boxster – The 986 series 1996-2004 (Long)
Porsche Boxster & Cayman – The 987 series (2004-2013) (Long)
Porsche Racing Cars – 1953 to 1975 (Long)
Porsche Racing Cars – 1976 to 2005 (Long)
Porsche – The Rally Story (Meredith)
Porsche: Three Generations of Genius (Meredith)
Powered by Porsche (Smith)
Preston Tucker & Others (Linde)
Rallye Sport Fords: The Inside Story (Moreton)
Runways & Racers (O'Neil)
RX-7 – Mazda's Rotary Engine Sportscar (Updated & Revised New Edition) (Long)
Sleeping Beauties USA – abandoned classic cars & trucks (Marek)
SM – Citroën's Maserati-engined Supercar (Long & Claverol)
Subaru Impreza: The Road Car And WRC Story (Long)
Tales from the Toolbox (Oliver)
Tatra – The Legacy of Hans Ledwinka, Updated & Enlarged Collector's Edition of 1500 copies (Margolius & Henry)
Toleman Story, The (Hilton)
Toyota Celica & Supra, The Book of Toyota's Sports Coupés (Long)
Toyota MR2 Coupés & Spyders (Long)
Two Summers – The Mercedes-Benz W196R Racing Car (Ackerson)
TWR Story, The – Group A (Hughes & Scott)
Unraced (Collins)
Volkswagen Bus Book, The (Bobbitt)
Volkswagen Bus or Van to Camper, How to Convert (Porter)
Volkswagens of the World (Glen)
VW Beetle Cabriolet – The full story of the convertible Beetle (Bobbitt)
VW Beetle – The Car of the 20th Century (Copping)
VW Bus – 40 Years of Splitties, Bays & Wedges (Copping)
VW Bus Book, The (Bobbitt)
VW Golf: Five Generations of Fun (Copping & Cservenka)
VW – The Air-cooled Era (Copping)
VW T5 Camper Conversion Manual (Porter)
VW Campers (Copping)
Volkswagen Type 3, The book of the – Concept, Design, International Production Models & Development (Glen)
Volvo Estate, The (Hollebone)
You & Your Jaguar XK8/XKR – Buying, Enjoying, Maintaining, Modifying – New Edition (Thorley)

www.veloce.co.uk

First published under ISBN 1-904788-19-X in 2002, and reprinted in 2004 by Veloce Publishing Limited, Veloce House, Parkway Farm Business Park, Middle Farm Way, Poundbury, Dorchester DT1 3AR, England Tel +44 (0)1305 260068 / Fax 01305 250479 / e-mail info@veloce.co.uk / web www.veloce.co.uk or www.velocebooks.com. Reprinted April 2018. ISBN: 978-1-787113-26-8 UPC: 6-36847-01326-4. © 2002, 2004 and 2018 Robert Ackerson and Veloce Publishing. All rights reserved. With the exception of quoting brief passages for the purpose of review, no part of this publication may be recorded, reproduced or transmitted by any means, including photocopying, without the written permission of Veloce Publishing Ltd. Throughout this book logos, model names and designations, etc, have been used for the purposes of identification, illustration and decoration. Such names are the property of the trademark holder as this is not an official publication. Readers with ideas for automotive books, or books on other transport or related hobby subjects, are invited to write to the editorial director of Veloce Publishing at the above address. British Library Cataloguing in Publication Data – A catalogue record for this book is available from the British Library. Typesetting, design and page make-up all by Veloce Publishing Ltd on Apple Mac. Printed and bound by CPI Group (UK) Ltd, Croydon, CR0 4YY.

CONTENTS

Acknowledgements 4
Introduction 5

1 KARMANN GHIA: A SHAPE EMERGES 6
Karmann Ghia and the Italian connection 6
A best-kept secret 8
The American connection 9
Getting it right 10
Body beautiful 17
Preparing for launch 21
Extending the range 22

2 EVOLUTION 24
First modifications 26
The Convertible arrives 27
Further changes 28
More power 30
A new direction - arrival of the Type 3 34
Post-1966 modifications 44
Type 1 cars continue 47
In retrospect 48
The Brazilian connection 48
Karmann Ghia in America 49

3 LIVING WITH A KARMANN GHIA 50
Driving a Karmann Ghia 51
Buying a Karmann Ghia 54
The pitfalls - and what to expect from the
    body beautiful 56
Running gear 64
Restoration - a brief guide 84
Interior trim 86
Replacement body sections 88
Luggage & engine compartment lids 90
Problems with the sun roof 90
Customising - and going faster 92

Appendix 1 Production figures 95
Appendix 2 Original specifications 97
Appendix 3 Colours 103
Appendix 4 At-a-glance chronology 105
Appendix 5 Specialists, suppliers, clubs
    & bibliography 106
Index 111

ACKNOWLEDGEMENTS

In writing this book I have had the good fortune to receive a lot of assistance and advice from many kind people, and I am very grateful to them all for giving up their time to make a special effort to help.

In particular, I should like to thank Martin McGarry for sparing me a large part of his time to talk about Karmann Ghias. I am also indebted to Martin for the use of his photographic collection and am even more grateful that he agreed to check my manuscript.

My appreciation also to Chris Spencer for his invaluable advice regarding all aspects of buying and living with a Karmann Ghia, and allowing me to photograph his coupé; Andrew Minney for reading through my text and spotting the gremlins the author always misses, and to Maria Cairnie, who has provided much help in the way of translation.

Thanks to Volkswagen-Audi Group UK for the use of photographic material and supply of historical information concerning the Volkswagen company. In addition, I would like to record the help provided by Renate Sanger, who so diligently sought archive photographs from the Volkswagen Museum at Wolfsburg.

As ever, I am grateful for all the help from the staff at the National Motor Museum; it seems this wonderful institution really does work miracles. Thank you all.

This book would not have been possible without the help of Rod and Judith at Veloce, who suggested the title to me in the first instance.

As always, my thanks to wife, Jean, who never fails to provide the necessary support and encouragement at just the right moment.

Malcolm Bobbitt

INTRODUCTION

Exactly what it is that makes a particular car a classic is not always easy to define. Some cars - those we remember from our youth - often mature to classic status, whilst others become legends in their own lifetimes. The Karmann Ghia is definitely in this latter category.

Although the Karmann Ghia shares a good deal of Volkswagen pedigree with the ubiquitous Beetle, any outward similarity is, perhaps, not immediately obvious, as it appears to have a greater kinship with the Porsche. Its very name is exotic-sounding, although this was not Wilhelm Karmann's intention. He had considered many names for his pretty coupé, none of which completely encapsulated the car's sweet lines. Finally, he teamed his own name with that of the house of Ghia and got just what he wanted.

The Karmann Ghia is aesthetically breathtaking; a perfect marriage of German thoroughness and Italian styling. It was no accident that the eminent styling studio of Ghia became involved with Karmann's project: Volkswagen was reluctant to back a venture for a sporting car when demand for the Beetle was already in excess of production capacity. Wilhelm Karmann, therefore, sought and received Ghia's help; a collaboration that Volkswagen carefully noted. The Karmann Ghia has an air of intrigue as the origin of its design is unclear, with both Carrozeria Ghia and Virgil Exner claiming the credit. The notion that the car's delightful styling emanated from America and not Italy is unthinkable to some. But take a look at Chrysler's Coupé D'Elegance, a design created by Ghia for Virgil Exner. Move the engine from the front to the rear and compare the result with the Karmann Ghia ...

For a car with a shape that suggests sheer sporting elegance, the Karmann Ghia is surprisingly sedate. Under that beautiful skin lies not a throbbing two or three litre engine, or even a highly tuned unit with the agility and speed of a thoroughbred racehorse. The running gear - pure Volkswagen Beetle - is, however, ingenious. Bespoke coachwork combined with proven and reliable mechanics make the Karmann Ghia a desirable car, and the exciting 2-seater alternative to the Beetle was handcrafted. Of course, Volkswagen owners would have already been well acquainted with Karmann as the Cabriolet was one of the most sought after Beetle variants.

The Karmann Ghia was especially appreciated in America, where something like 40 per cent of production was exported, particularly to California. Even with the elementary air-cooled engine, a fraction the size of some American power units, the car was respected and enjoyed. Luckily, the sheer number of cars that went to the States - together with the climate there - means that many survive today. Along with the familiar Karmann Ghia there appeared an equally refined Convertible, although this was built in considerably fewer numbers. An even rarer Karmann Ghia - based on the Volkswagen Type 3 - never enjoyed the same popularity.

The Karmann Ghia today has a large following. Its beguiling figure, mated to rugged Volkswagen running gear - makes it much more than a classic: it is a true legend and this is its story.

Malcolm Bobbitt

1
KARMANN GHIA: A SHAPE EMERGES

It is a measure of the Karmann Ghia's success that, within a year of its launch, production figures had more than doubled. It had originally been planned to produce 20 cars a day, which would have resulted in between 300 and 400 cars a month being delivered. This was the summer of 1955 but, by the end of 1956, something approaching 1000 cars were leaving the factory gates each month.

The Karmann Ghia is certainly one of the most charismatic cars of the post-war era, and it encapsulates an exceptional recipe of excellent fundamental engineering and exquisite styling. Its pedigree is there for all to see: Volkswagen precision, with roots far deeper in automobile history than Wolfsburg production, and Italian elegance provided by coachbuilder Ghia of Turin. And all neatly packaged by Karmann's Osnabrück craftsmen.

The name Karmann is, of course, synonymous with Volkswagen, as Wilhelm Karmann was instrumental, at almost the start of that company's post-war car production, in producing for Wolfsburg the Cabriolet version of the ubiquitous Beetle. The link with Carrozeria Ghia resulted in the outstanding Karmann Ghia Coupé, an Italian-styled alternative to the established convertible already on offer.

News of the Karmann Ghia was first reported in July 1955 when it was announced that a Coupé body was to be available for the Volkswagen at Osnabrück, which was already supplying the Beetle's convertible body. Whereas both the standard Beetle and its convertible stablemate boasted of being 4-seater cars, the new Coupé did not pretend to be anything other than a 2+2. The equally elegant Karmann Ghia Cabriolet joined the Coupé some three years later in 1958.

In America - considered probably the car's most important export market - the Karmann Ghia was immediately accepted; the only pertinent criticism seems to be that the car was initially in short supply. It quickly galloped to the top of the import charts, making it the most popular foreign-produced car. In California the Beetle ranked 7th as the most wanted car: quite an achievement in the land of plenty ...

Volkswagen was not alone in looking westward across the Atlantic to North America: both Renault and Fiat regarded the United States as a challenging market, and were considerably successful with their small models. Renault's 4CV heralded the invasion of America, followed by the Dauphine and the pretty Caravelle. Fiat sent shiploads of 600s across the Atlantic, which were later joined by the sporting 850 variants, Cars such as the Volvo 1800 sports Coupé and BMW 700 were, perhaps, not as successful, whilst British manufacturers made a vague attempt at penetrating the American market with, amongst others, the Austin Atlantic.

Karmann Ghia and the Italian connection

As well as producing the convertible variant of the Beetle, Wilhelm Karmann had aspirations to produce a coachbuilt sporting car using standard Volkswagen running gear, but with totally unique body styling. The shape of such a car would be sleek and sensuous, a design in its own right and not merely a conversion of an existing model. Although Wilhelm Karmann died in 1952 at the age of 88, and was therefore denied the opportunity of seeing his dream materialise in its

One of the first Karmann Ghia brochures, in this case Dutch. News of the car was announced to the press during July 1955. (Courtesy National Motor Museum)

definitive form, his son, also Wilhelm, who inherited the family business and became its chief shareholder, ensured the dream's fruition.

Efforts to pave the way for a true sports car commenced in 1950 when Wilhelm Karmann's son first discussed such a proposal with Heinz Nordhoff. There is evidence that Nordhoff was not particularly impressed, his seeming disinterest stemming from the fact that the Beetle was outstandingly successful and production capacity at Wolfsburg about to be overstretched. With the decision already taken to sub-contract the Cabriolet Beetle, there might have appeared to Nordhoff little point in creating another product whose potential for success could well be questionable.

Heinz Nordhoff's rebuff did not deter Karmann and he tried again and again to persuade Nordhoff to accept his idea. Nordhoff did allow Karmann to submit designs and plans to Wolfsburg, which were then evaluated by Ludwig Boehner (in charge of product development at the Volkswagen factory) and Dr Karl Feuereissen (head of the company's sales and service division), who, together, advised Heinz Nordhoff of the viability or otherwise of a proposed new creation. In addition to drawings, Wilhelm Karmann had scale models made up at Osnabrück, but each time a new design was submitted it failed to secure complete Volkswagen approval.

Wilhelm Karmann's plans at the outset had centred around a stylish Cabriolet and not a Coupé. It is understandable why a Cabriolet was initially envisaged, given that this type of body styling was Karmann's speciality and the company was already producing the convertible Beetle. At the time, Karmann was also producing a convertible version of the DKW, of which almost 7000 examples were built, and a Kombi version of Ford's Taunus, which accounted for some 9000 cars. Had a Coupé been presented to Wolfsburg first, the outcome may have been entirely different.

An important factor in designing a suitable Volkswagen-based sports car was the chassis itself: in his endeavours Wilhelm Karmann had found it difficult to use the platform as a successful base, due almost entirely to its restrictive dimensions, a factor that would become particularly relevant.

Development of the Karmann Ghia took something of a twist when the younger Wilhelm Karmann involved Luigi Segre in the project. Segre, who

Prototype Karmann Ghia exhibited at the Karmann collection. (Courtesy Martin McGarry)

was commercial director of Carrozzeria Ghia, had become well acquainted with Karmann as a result of both companys' interest in the motor industry. On a particular occasion at one of Europe's motor shows, Karmann was able to discuss his ideas in some depth with Segre and asked him, almost out of desperation, whether his company might prepare a design that would meet with Volkswagen approval. Segre showed more than a degree of interest in the project but did not make a firm commitment to offer his company's assistance or his own expertise on that occasion.

Luigi Segre would, of course, have been aware of the suitability of the Volkswagen chassis and running gear for a sports car; Ferdinand Porsche's own efforts in developing the Volkswagen were well known and the Porsche 356 sports Coupé and Cabriolet, which was based upon the Volkswagen principle, had already been launched to much acclaim. The first that Wilhelm Karmann Senior knew of Luigi Segre's level of interest in his project was when he was invited by Ghia to take a look at something that 'might interest him' ...

What had actually happened was that Segre, on returning to Turin after his initial conversation with Karmann, was to obtain a standard Beetle from the Wolfsburg production line. This was not as straightforward as it might seem as, quite simply, a car was not available. It was obvious a more devious route would be necessary in order to obtain a car and Segre approached Charles Ladouche who, at that time, was concessionaire in France for both Volkswagen and Chrysler. Ladouche, who was known to Wilhelm Karmann, obliged and the car was collected from France during the early part of 1953 and driven to Turin by Gian Paolo Boano, son of Mario Felice Boano. The fact that Ladouche was involved with Chrysler had a bearing on the future of Karmann Ghia, as is revealed in the next chapter.

Luigi Segre, who had plans drawn up at his Ghia studios, had the car prepared by the autumn of 1953, the prototype having taken just five months to build. It was while Wilhelm Karmann was visiting France and staying in Paris that he received the all-important call from Segre. Luigi Segre had the prototype car shipped from the Ghia studios at Turin to Paris, where he and Charles Ladouche presented the design to Karmann. Karmann was amazed at what greeted him; not only was the prototype car beautiful beyond all doubt, but perfectly embodied the theme he had envisaged. What was all the more striking was that Segre's offering was a Coupé and not a convertible, the latter being the only body form Karmann had considered up to that point.

Luigi Segre had given the project to Mario Boano, not as an official contract but as a means of arriving at a design Karmann might consider for future production. Boano had already been heavily involved in producing some spectacular designs for the Italian motor industry, and some of the features found on the definitive car are reminiscent of the Ghia-bodied Alfa-Romeo 6C 2500S and the 1900C Coupé. In developing the Karmann Ghia, Mario Boano also enlisted the help of his son, Gian Paolo, together with Sergio Coggiola who had recently joined the Ghia company. Although Mario Boano supervised the whole affair, much of the detailed drawings were undertaken by Sergio Coggiola. Coggiola's involvement in the project was fortuitous, as he later became chief engineer at Ghia with special responsibility for Karmann's affairs.

How the Karmann Ghia got its ultimate styling is a tortuous essay in mystery and intrigue; many stories abound in the intricate patchwork of automotive history. What makes the issue all the more controversial is the fact that most of the people involved in the affair are now no longer alive ...

A best-kept secret
Early development of the Karmann Ghia was one of the motor industry's best-kept secrets: not only did Wilhelm Karmann refrain from telling even his closest colleagues of his discussions with Luigi Segre of Carrozzeria Ghia, but the prototype car was transported around Europe, when need be, concealed within an armoured truck!

Charles Ladouche, who had interests in Volkswagen and Chrysler, was involved in the conception and birth of Wilhelm Karmann's dream car from the outset, along with Luigi Segre and the small but dedicated design team at Carrozzeria Ghia. Volkswagen was kept from knowing of Ghia's involvement with Karmann, although Luigi Segre would almost surely have been aware of Karmann's efforts with Volkswagen before he approached the Turin coachbuilder. Even after Ladouche and Segre presented Ghia's prototype car to Wilhelm Karmann in Paris, it was taken surreptitiously to Osnabrück and concealed in a part of the factory safe from prying eyes.

Once the overall styling was decided, the question of how to adapt the design to the Beetle's restrictive chassis dimensions arose. With this resolved, Heinz Nordhoff and Dr Karl Feuereisen were invited to Osnabrück to view the creation. Nordhoff's reaction was immediate and without hesitation: he realised that what he saw undoubtedly had serious potential for Volkswagen.

The American connection
The exact origin of the Karmann Ghia's styling has always been unclear, and intrigue surrounds the design's key players. Rumours and suppositions abound, but just how the undeniably attractive appearance was arrived at will never be known for sure.

Luigi Segre's early involvement with Charles Ladouche is the first indication that the Chrysler Corporation was connected with the affair. Not only was Ladouche the French agent for Chrysler, but Segre had been involved with the Detroit company, responsible for the styling of an exclusive Coupé. The D'Eelegance, as the Coupé became known, was eventually marketed in France as the GS1 and sold through Ladouche's company, Société France Motors. The cars were built, with the permission of Chrysler, by Ghia in Turin; an association which resulted in some 400 vehicles being delivered.

There was more than just a hint of similarity between the overall styling of the D'Elegance and the Karmann Ghia, although the Chrysler's front-engine configuration meant that its frontal appearance was different and, naturally, the Karmann Ghia was considerably smaller. Both cars shared characteristics such as a large glass area, sharply-raked windscreen and front wing-tops that swept back in an arc, diving to a swage line low on the doors before rising quickly over the rear wheelarches. The D'Elegance's front-mounted engine allowed the car to have fast-back styling, which the Karmann Ghia did not have.

What is of importance is that Ghia was already producing Chrysler's D'Elegance at Turin before Wilhelm Karmann was shown his prototype car. It is questionable why Segre and Ladouche went to the effort of transporting the Karmann Ghia prototype to Paris when it almost certainly would have been far easier for Karmann to travel to Turin. Had Karmann visited Ghia's studio at Turin he could not have missed seeing the Chrysler car in production...

Two leading figures in the affair were Mario Felice Boano and Virgil Exner. Boano, who was head of the Ghia styling house, had already been involved with Chrysler by showing Exner some drawings he had prepared based upon a Plymouth chassis. The invitation to design the prospective vehicle had come from C. B. Thomas, Chrysler's vice president, in 1951, as the car would have been intended as part of the company's export drive. European manufacturers were already queuing at the doors of Carrozzeria Ghia, seeking to produce a specialist alternative to their bread-and-butter models. In his designs Boano embodied all that was current in Italian styling at the turn of the decade. The 'Plymouth affair' was a direct result of Luigi Segre visiting America in an attempt to develop Ghia's business acumen.

Chrysler's corporate styling was largely the responsibility of Vigil Exner. Exner had worked for Chrysler since 1950 but, before that, had been deeply involved with the Raymond Loewy Studios at South Bend, Indiana. His career at the Loewy Studios had involved Exner in the production of the famous and striking Studebaker Champion of 1947, the car which heralded an all-new approach to American auto styling. Chrysler's image changed dramatically once Virgil Exner had time to get established at Detroit: Henry King, the company's chief stylist, had retired, so Exner's influence was allowed to grow. Softer lines incorporating curvaceously-styled front wings, prominent rear wings and huge wrap-around rear windows were all Exner trademarks. Gone also from Detroit was K. T. Keller, Chrysler's President, and with him went the bulbous styling of the '40s.

Luigi Segre had had dealings with Virgil Exner before the Coupé D'Elegance affair. A prototype car, the K310, had followed on the heels of Ghia's preparation of the Plymouth, which had been codenamed XX500. The K310 was a joint effort between Segre and Exner, inspired by Segre and valued by Exner as an example of Ghia's styling ability.

Chrysler's Coupé D'Elegance - Virgil Exner claimed that Ghia used his design for the Karmann Ghia. (Courtesy National Motor Museum)

The link between Karmann, Chrysler and Carrozzeria Ghia, therefore, makes it impossible to confidently state from where the Karmann Ghia's styling originated. Virgil Exner certainly claimed that the design presented to Karmann was his and not Ghia's. It would appear that, in designing the D'Elegance, a clay model had been prepared as well as drawings and sent to Ghia at Turin for the company to work on. Exner's own view is that Ghia was having problems finding a suitable design to present to Wilhelm Karmann and, almost as a last resort, scaled down his own design for the D'Elegance. Virgil Exner further claimed that Ghia altered the fine detail in accordance with the stylist's established hallmarks.

Ghia's own interpretation is, as can be expected, quite different. Certainly it is known that Ghia was working on the D'Elegance at the time the Karmann Ghia prototype was being created, but then, of course, the styling company would have been working on a number of different projects. The fact that the end product bore a certain resemblance to the Exner creation was attributed to current styling trends which were being pursued on both sides of the Atlantic.

Whatever actually happened behind closed doors will probably never be fully understood. What *is* known, however, is that the Karmann design which emerged from Turin was immediately pronounced a classic.

Getting it right

Only after Carrozzeria Ghia had supplied the prototype design to Karmann and negotiated a suitable fee did Wilhelm Karmann involve his colleagues in the project. The

Shift the engine to the rear and round-off the nose: there are those who claim that the D'Elegance was the basis for the Karmann Ghia design. (Courtesy National Motor Museum)

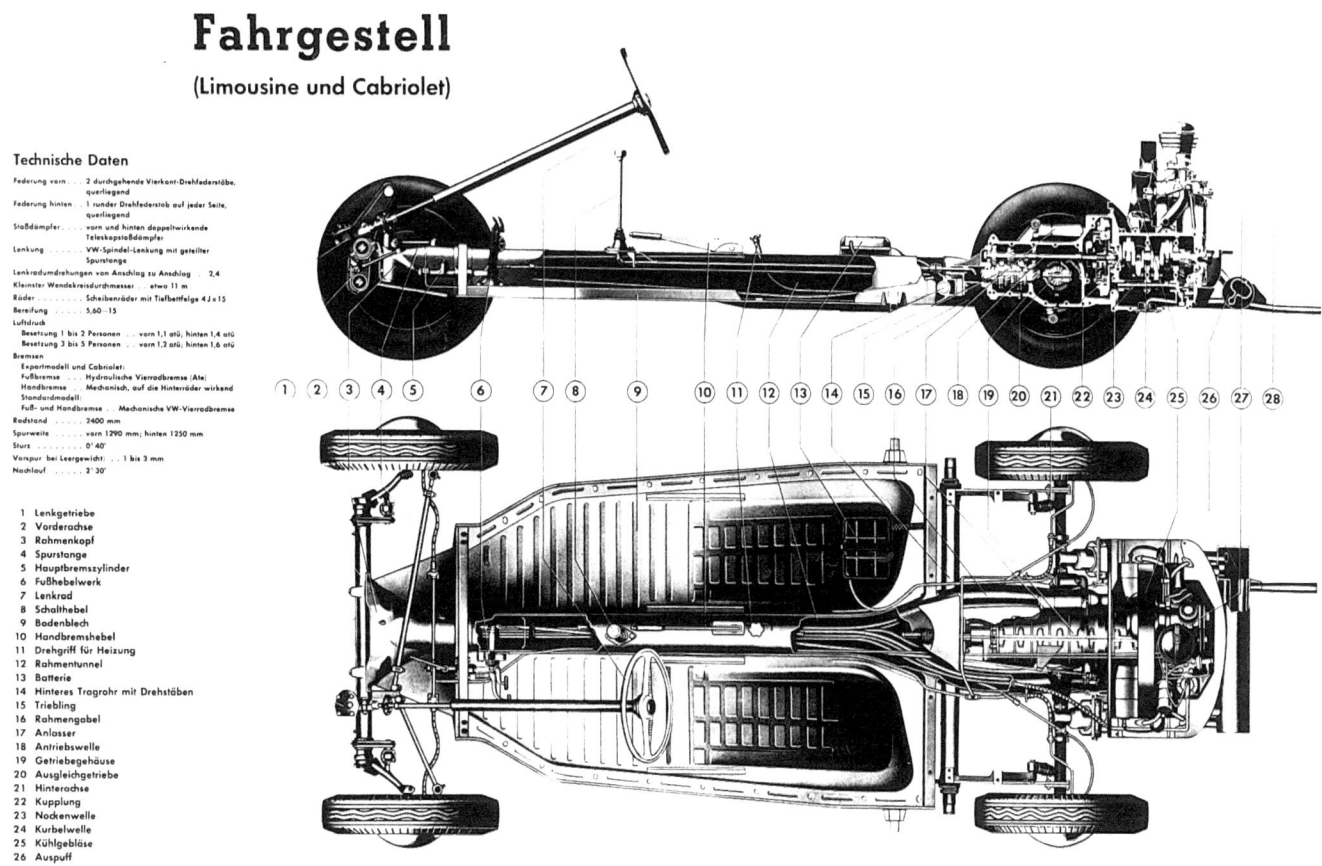

The Volkswagen Beetle chassis was used as a basis for the Karmann Ghia. (Courtesy Stiftung AutoMuseum Volkswagen)

revelation of Karmann's behind-the-scenes activities came, quite likely, as something of a shock, although the reasons for the secrecy were understood.

There was every reason for Wilhelm Karmann to keep the project secret from other manufacturers and coachbuilders. Apart from there being a need, in Karmann's view, for keeping the matter of Ghia's involvement from Wolfsburg in case the plan was vetoed by Volkswagen, Karmann was convinced that, should the project fail to materialise, his Osnabrück workforce might suffer some demoralisation.

Ghia's involvment ended, in effect, once Karmann accepted the prototype design. All further evaluation and testing, along with detail design changes, was for Karmann to organize. The length of time between the prototype being delivered to Osnabrück and Heinz Nordhoff and Dr Feuereisen seeing the finished article was only a matter of weeks; Ghia supplied Karmann with the car in September and on 16th November 1953 VW's Nordhoff was pledging unequivocal support for the car's future.

To get the Karmann Ghia into production would obviously take time; a considerable amount of work was necessary to perfect the mechanical design and to carry out the tooling-up process. Wilhelm Karmann, together with Luigi Segre and Charles Ladouche, were keen to have the car ready for the Paris Salon in October 1954 and thereby maximise its success. The Volkswagen management team, cautious as ever, was less than sure about pushing ahead at such speed and preferred to wait until the autumn shows scheduled for the following year. The extra time would not only ensure that the design had been mechanically perfected, but there would be an adequate stock of cars to sell instead of adding to an ever-lengthening waiting list.

The initial post-prototype development period began with a whole series of intensive discussions between Volkswagen and Karmann engineers. The immediate, and most important, task to accomplish was that of adapting the Beetle's chassis to Ghia's design; not easy due to the Volkswagen's inherently narrow platform. To this end some four or five test cars were constructed at Osnabrück, each destined for an arduous and intense testing evaluation.

Usually a motor manufacturer would produce tens of test cars when developing a new model; not so Karmann, whose limited resources did not allow such an outlay. The

Publicity pictures of the chassis of the original Volkswagen. (Courtesy Stiftung AutoMuseum Volkswagen)

fact that a maximum of five cars were built for test purposes just goes to illustrate Karmann's somewhat limited resources, compared to volume production manufacturers. It does, however, confirm that the company was, in its own terms, committed in no small way to achieving engineering excellence.

The Beetle's chassis, whilst an ideal base for coachbuilders, did have its limitations for specialised coachwork, and it was this that Karmann engineers tackled initially with the help of Wolfsburg engineers. The chassis had not presented any problems in connection with the Beetle Cabriolet as both Karmann's offering, and Hebmüller's, were very closely related to the original Saloon version. Few chassis offered as much as that of the Volkswagen; a fact borne out by the number of variants and one-off designs which have appeared throughout the car's lifespan.

Essentially, the concept of the Volkswagen Beetle chassis is extremely simple. In reality it consists of two floorpans constructed from pressed steel, connected by means of a central backbone. This is a development from the earliest prototype cars whose chassis were built with wooden floorboards. What is important to understand is that the rigidity of the vehicle is not derived entirely from the chassis spine as it relies equally as much on the body for strength. This is substantiated by problems quickly discovered with the early Cabriolets, which suffered rigidity problems stemming from the fact that they were based on ordinary Saloons that had not only had their roofs removed, but were left without any compensating reinforcement.

One of the main advantages of the Volkswagen chassis is the ease with which it can be separated from the body. In essence, body and chassis are held together by a series of bolts, which number some 30 in total; to undo these is a relatively straightforward process requiring a simple set of tools. Once the body has been removed it is quite possible to propel a chassis under its own power.

Apart from acting as a backbone to the chassis, the central spine also housed the car's control gear, such as gearchange linkage, handbrake mechanism, accelerator, clutch and choke cables; the fuel line was also located within the backbone but instead of the pipes for the rear brakes being housed within the tunnel, they were positioned alongside it. This principle was also later used in 1955 by Fiat in the rear-engined 600 model which replaced the conventionally driven Topolino.

At the rear of the Volkswagen platform the backbone is divided into two distinct forks, one extending each side of the gearbox assembly. This design of chassis was not entirely new as its origin can be traced back to 1933, when it was first devised for the Tracta.

The front of the gearbox is attached to the hub of the fork while the fork's two prongs terminate alongside the gearbox bellhousing, so forming mountings for the transmission unit. The engine is mounted directly to the gearbox and has no further mountings as such.

When first produced, the Beetle's suspension represented a huge leap forward in technology; the rather primitive springing found on most contemporary cars was replaced by torsion bars and all four wheels were independently sprung. Ride quality was undoubtedly improved and made smooth work of the most uneven surfaces. Little was to change with the Karmann Ghia: at the front, parallel trailing arms and torsion bars were enclosed within transversely mounted tubes, one above the other. The rear suspension again had torsion bars which, this time, were contained in single tubes installed ahead of the gearbox and placed across the chassis. A single trailing arm on each side, attached to the hub assembly and swing axle, formed the springing.

DER MOTOR DES KDF=WAGENS

Der KdF=Wagen hat einen Vierzylinder=Boxermotor, der im Heck des Wagens untergebracht ist. Die Zylinder arbeiten im Viertakt und haben einen Hubraum von 986 ccm. Bei einer normalen Drehzahl von 3000 p. M. leistet der Wagen 23,5 PS, das entspricht einer Stundengeschwindigkeit von rund 100 km.

Der Motor hat Luftkühlung. Im Luftführungsgehäuse ist der Ölkühler untergebracht, der so bemessen ist, daß niedrige Öltemperaturen auch bei größter Beanspruchung stets für eine ausreichende Schmierung aller Schmierstellen des Motors sorgen. Hierdurch wird die erstaunliche Autobahnfestigkeit des KdF=Wagens erreicht, die Höchstgeschwindigkeit gleich Dauergeschwindigkeit sein läßt. Die Kühlung wird nicht wie bei einem vorn liegenden Motor von der Geschwindigkeit des Fahrzeuges beeinflußt, sondern hängt von der Drehzahl des Motors ab. Dadurch wird in gebirgigem Gelände selbst bei geringer Geschwindigkeit und höchster Motorbeanspruchung eine Überhitzung restlos vermieden.

Ventile:	kopfgesteuert.
Zündung:	Batterie=Lichtmaschinenzündung.
Batterie:	6 Volt.
Lichtmaschine:	spannungsregulierend.
Anlasser:	mit Ritzel auf Schwungrad wirkend.
Vergaser:	Fallstromvergaser.
Kraftstoff-Förderung:	entsprechend den bestehenden Vorschriften sind Motor und Benzintank voneinander getrennt untergebracht. Eine Kraftstoffpumpe fördert das Benzin vom Tank zum Motor.
Kupplung:	Einscheibentrockenkupplung.
Getriebe:	4 Vorwärtsgänge, 1 Rückwärtsgang, 3. und 4. Gang geräuscharm. Die Höchstgeschwindigkeit des 1. Ganges ist 20 km, des 2. Ganges 40 km, des 3. Ganges 65 km in der Stunde.
Ölverbrauch:	normal nur bei Ölwechsel (2,5 Liter für etwa 2500 Kilometer).
Kraftstoff-Verbrauch:	6 bis 7 Liter Benzin auf 100 Kilometer je nach Fahrweise und Gelände.

Der Motor des KdF=Wagens zeichnet sich durch leichte Zugänglichkeit zu seinen Einzelteilen aus, der Motorausbau und -einbau ist in kürzester Frist durchzuführen, man braucht dazu etwa je 10 Min. Der Motor des KdF=Wagens ist so konstruiert, daß alle Sorten Benzin des In- und Auslandes gefahren werden können.

> **Und die Reparaturen?**
> Es werden neuartige Wege beschritten werden, die Ausgaben für Reparaturen, wenn sie notwendig werden sollten, so niedrig wie möglich zu halten. Eine Vereinfachung ist schon dadurch gegeben, daß die einzelnen Teile des KdF=Wagens, auch der Motor, gut zugänglich sind und ebenso leicht montiert werden können. Ferner werden eine ganze Reihe Austauschteile vorbereitet. Bei größeren Unfällen tritt die Versicherung in Kraft.

The engine compartment as shown in the original KdF Wagen brochure. (Author's collection)

Final checks before leaving the factory. An original picture from KdF Wagen publicity. (Author's collection)

The Volkswagen engine and gearbox followed the relatively simple engineering techniques applied to the chassis construction. Positioned over the rear axle, and designed to provide maximum traction under all circumstances, the engine - an air-cooled, 4-cylinder boxer unit - was built with long life in mind. A two-piece magnesium-alloy crankcase with cast-iron cylinders, aluminium pistons and forged connecting rods was a recipe for success. Along with this was a 4-bearing forged-steel crankshaft with camshaft driven directly from it and operating entirely within the crankcase.

Air-cooled engines, in the main, incorporate an oil cooler within their design and the Volkswagen is no exception. To provide cooling, a large fan, which was mounted directly onto the dynamo and driven by a belt attached to the end of the crankshaft, forced air around the engine, itself surrounded by metal ducting to direct the airflow. Although efficient, air-cooled engines can cause cabin heating difficulties and both the Volkswagen Saloon and Karmann Ghia suffered in this respect. In the Karmann Ghia, air passing over the engine's cooling fins was warmed before being blown through the body sills to filter into the cabin through vents at floor level, as well as to the base of the windscreen. This worked well enough if the engine was clean; if, however, oil or dirt was allowed to build up around the engine, fumes and oily smoke would almost certainly permeate the cabin with nasty consequences. Fortunately, this system of heating was discontinued after 1963 when heat exchangers ensured warmed fresh air entered the car.

Reliability rather than performance was the long-term requirement of the air-cooled boxer engine. That being the case, the Beetle's almost lethargic performance can be understood, as too can the number of tuning conversions which, although not specified by Volkswagen as standard equipment or a factory option, soon became popular! Replacing the simple downdraught carburettor with even the most basic

In 1955, the Karmann Ghia's styling was breathtakingly different to that of its contemporaries. (Author's collection)

tuning kit allowed noticeably increased power output, and without too much effort it was possible to increase it by something like a third.

From the beginning of production 4-speed gearboxes were standard equipment, but it was not until 1952 that synchromesh was fitted to 2nd, 3rd and 4th ratios on export models. For the standard model, owners had to continue to make do with the familiar 'crash' gearbox. The braking system initially relied upon cable-operated drums for all models and it was only with the appearance of the de-luxe, otherwise known as the export version, that hydraulic brakes became available. Even as late as 1962 the standard model retained outdated cable brakes but, as far as the Karmann Ghia is concerned, the car's mechanical specification was based entirely upon the export chassis.

The Karmann Ghia's single-circuit hydraulic braking system was quite conventional: the all-round 9 inch (230mm) drum brakes were fitted with a leading and trailing shoe at each wheel and could be manually adjusted by a clamp nut on the rear of the drum; the handbrake, operated by a lever between the seats, acted on the rear wheels only.

The solution, as far as adapting the Beetle chassis to the Karmann Ghia was concerned, was to modify the platform to successfully accommodate Ghia's styling. This was achieved by increasing the platform width by 80mm each side and adding reinforcement to the side members, which were built

The Karmann Ghia's doors were devoid of window frames and, at approximately a metre wide, allowed easy access. (Author's collection)

into place beneath the doors.

These modifications enabled the cabin of the Karmann Ghia to be radically different to that of the Beetle. The seats were lower, altering considerably the driving position and necessitating a change in the angle of the steering column. As a result, the gearchange lever also had to be shortened.

A further modification was the adoption of an anti-roll bar at the front of the car; this amounted to a 12 inch (150mm) stabilizer being attached to the front suspension, linking the two lower trailing arms and anchored in rubber bushes. The ride and handling benefited greatly from this modification which was not added to the Beetle until 1960; the most noticeable improvement was the absence of oversteer, a most typical feature of early Beetles, and elimination of the rather harsh vertical movements of the suspension, mostly experienced on uneven roads at lower speeds. At last the driver could confidently take the car through bends on wet roads without fear of losing rear wheel grip.

There would seem to be some

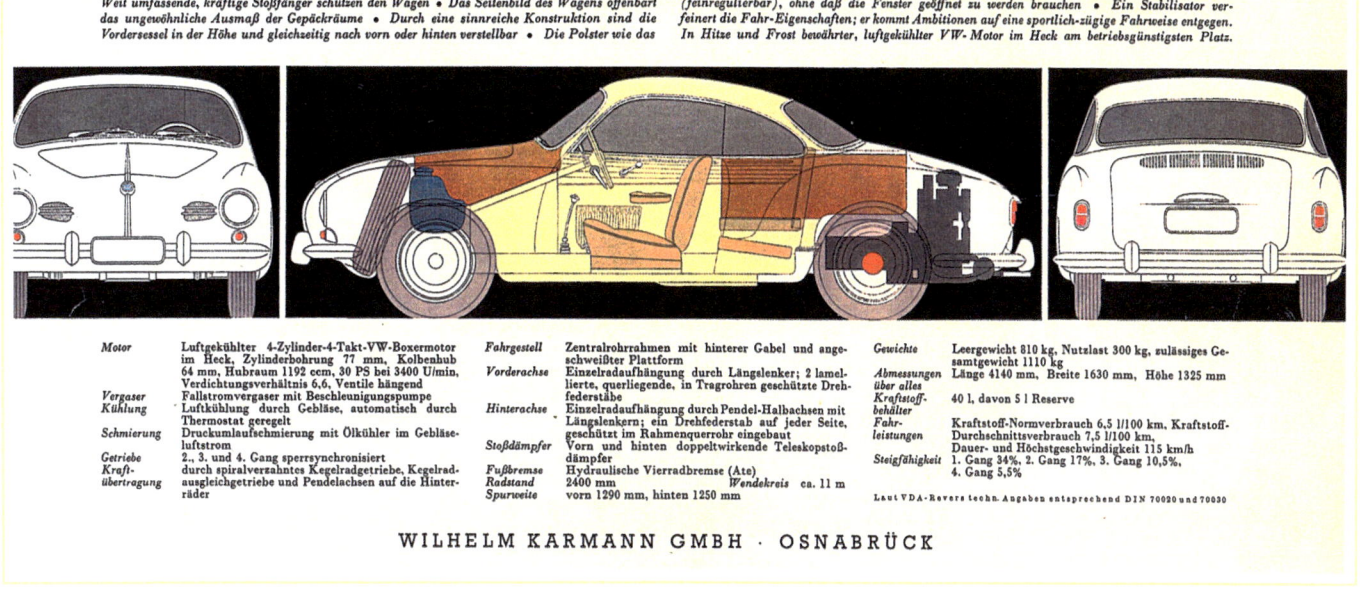

The Karmann Ghia's layout is graphically detailed in this German brochure dating from about 1956. (Courtesy National Motor Museum)

confusion concerning what type of steering mechanism the Karmann Ghia used. From the outset it was of the worm and nut type and utilised unequal length track rods and a transverse link. The steering has often been praised for its precision and lightness, due entirely to its Porsche-designed steering box. This was updated in 1962 to a worm and roller unit which improved the steering still further. Some road test information shows the steering to be of the rack and pinion type, but this is quite erroneous.

The lower profile of the Karmann Ghia, as opposed to the rather upright stance of the Beetle, necessitated some shoe-horning of the engine and transmission unit in order to make it fit under the engine compartment cover. There being no need to alter the way the unit sat over the rear axle, the modification extended only as far as replacing the usual air filter with the type used by the Type 2 VW Transporter. Instead of being positioned at the top of the engine, the filter could be relocated to the left hand side of the unit. The greater width of the Karmann Ghia also enabled the battery to be housed in the engine compartment, to the right of the engine, instead of under the rear seat as on the Beetle, a position which was less than satisfactory but necessary in view of the Saloon's limited engine compartment space.

Like the Beetle, the original Karmann Ghia used 6-volt electrics, a practice more common in Europe than in Britain. The limitations of a 6-volt system will be understood and 12-volt electrics were later adopted.

From the outset the Karmann Ghia was built around standard Volkswagen mechanicals, albeit in export specification. This determined that the more powerful 1192cc engine available from 1954 was employed rather than the original 1131cc unit, which had been introduced for all post-war production cars from 1945. A point of interest is that the 1939 Volkswagen had been specified with an engine of 986cc and originally it was the *Schwimmwagen* which first received the 1131cc power unit. As in the case of the Beetle, the Karmann Ghia retained the familiar layout of the front-mounted fuel tank and spare wheel ahead of the luggage compartment and between the front wheels. The Beetle always suffered by having very restricted carrying capacity under the front bonnet, a feature not much improved in the Karmann Ghia although accepted by enthusiasts as characteristic of the car.

To suit the sporting image of the Karmann Ghia it was necessary to lower the Beetle's suspension. This was accomplished by modifications to the torsion bar set and shock absorbers. Overall, the Karmann Ghia utilised the same basic chassis layout and similar components to the standard Volkswagen but, nevertheless, modifications amounted to several hundred differences, most of which could be considered very minor.

Such was the excellence of Ghia's styling that the initial design remained largely unaltered throughout development and into production. Minor detail modifications were made, the most noticeable being to the frontal styling which originally had appeared much more bullet-like than the definitive production car. Initially, the car did not have fresh-air intakes

Reuters' illustrations often overstated a car's features; even so, the Karmann Ghia is delightfully styled, earning it the accolade of one of the most beautiful cars ever built. (Courtesy National Motor Museum)

and the indicator lamps were inset in the headlamps, which themselves were slightly different.

Frontal styling was altered by some smoothing-out of the deeply curved front wings which helped to soften the appearance of the headlamps. A revised bumper, which now extended the full width of the car, also incorporated overriders that provided added protection. By relocating the indicators from their inboard position to immediately under the headlights, and adding fresh-air vents to the front panel, the car's appearance was considerably improved. A clever and effective styling touch was shaping the fresh-air vents to echo the overall curvaceousness of the car.

The prototype car had been designed with windscreen wipers which were pivoted at the outer ends of the scuttle; sweeping inwards, the wiper arms settled at the base of the windscreen in a 'cross-over' position. On the definitive car these were replaced with the more conventional arrangement.

The rear styling also received minor detail changes: vents each side of the numberplate were not entirely in keeping with the overall image and were dispensed with. Too intrusive were the cooling louvres punched into the engine compartment lid, and a less conspicuous design, which didn't reduce airflow, was found.

The design ultimately offered to Karmann was the third of three prototype styling evaluations by Ghia. All three exercises were strikingly similar in concept, each showing only superficial variations on a theme. The first displayed sharp-edged styling resulting in high-mounted twin headlamps and slab-sided rear wings which swept upwards to reveal a suggestion of tail fins. The front wings of the second prototype were more prominent but encompassed single headlights; vestigial rear wings, as on the definitive car, had high-mounted rear lamps.

Both Karmann and Ghia were attracted to the idea of a full 4-seater Coupé. Development of this idea had resulted in a couple of prototype cars being built which, in the event, were not entirely satisfactory. The styling of the cabin and the engine compartment

Inside the Karmann factory. The lack of large presses resulted in largely labour-intensive assembly of many small body panels. On the left-hand line can be seen Beetle Cabriolets. (Author's collection)

could not be successfully consolidated with the result that the overall design was considered too clumsy. The project was put aside, perhaps to be reconsidered later: in the event it never materialised.

Body beautiful

The Karmann Ghia quickly earned the accolade of the most beautiful Volkswagen ever built, and was certainly considered by many to be possibly one of the most gracious cars of the fifties. Not only did it have Italian panache - which is ironic, considering the possibilities of the American connection - it also featured the excellence and steadfastness of German engineering.

The potential for success of the Karmann Ghia was apparent even at the time the car was undergoing trials. Much of the testing of the prototype cars was carried out on the French and Italian Riviera and Luigi Segre had a passion for trying out the car whenever possible. Everywhere the car went it was the centre of much attention and it was only because it was without badges that its identity was kept secret.

There is little doubt that Heinz Nordhoff and Dr Karl Feuereisen might have wondered whether Ghia's styling details were a little too adventurous for Wolfsburg. After all, split front bumpers and a prominent nose design flew in the face of convention, which was probably the reason for the minor restyling that occurred. For all the car's exotic appearance there was, apparently, little concern expressed at some of the more unusual features: frameless windows, pillarless doors, remotely controlled catches for boot and bonnet and push-button door locks were all happily accepted.

Construction of the Karmann Ghia was a largely labour-intensive operation. Not only was the Osnabrück concern relatively small by motor industry standards, but Karmann would not normally have been associated with high volume production, especially with a vehicle of such complexity. Due to the nature of Karmann's usual manufacturing output, the company did not have the large presses normally required for large-scale production. Reliance was, therefore, put upon existing presses which, by their nature, had limited capability and were designed to form relatively small panels. Specially-designed jigs were used to secure each body panel until the entire structure had been fitted in place and then welded or bolted together.

In tooling-up for the Karmann Ghia (which, by this time, had been designated Type 143 in the somewhat obscure Volkswagen model identification system), the engineers at Osnabrück embarked upon the exacting task of fabricating dyes for each body panel. Initially, the guide for each dye had to be painstakingly produced out of hardwood to

The Karmann Ghia's 2+2 seating configuration meant two children could be fairly comfortably carried. With the rear seat folded, luggage capacity was considerably increased. (Author's collection)

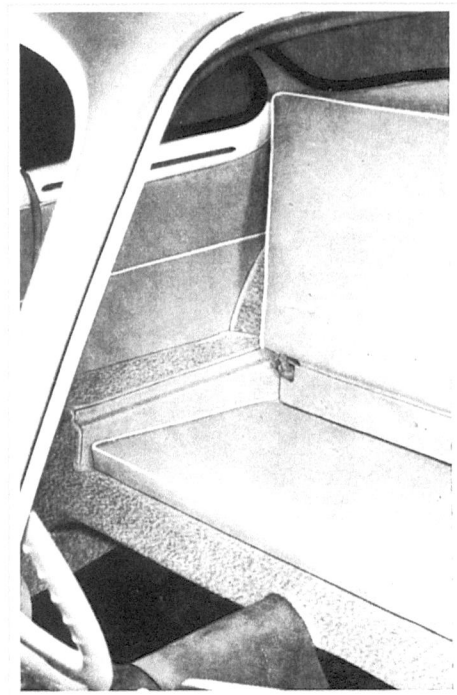

meticulous measurements before being transformed into steel. Only when the dye was to precise size and form was it toughened in order to withstand the rigours of the production processes.

Rather than being made up of larger pressings, the body was constructed from a myriad of small panels, the largest of which were the front and rear wings, bonnet, roof, engine compartment lid and the two doors. The remaining panels, of which there were many, were built up from individual pieces welded together; to achieve a fine surface all irregularities had to filled with lead before being smoothed out. As an example of the intensity of the operation, the front of the car was made up of no less than five separate panels, each welded, filled and smoothed to enable the fine contours to be achieved.

As for the doors, these appeared simple in their construction but, in fact, were exactly the opposite. Whilst needing to be lightweight there was, nonetheless, the need for strength, a fundamental requirement in respect of the frameless window design. Strength was built in by joining the inner and outer panels in such a way that, even after a lifetime of being opened and closed, the structural reliability of the door would not in any way be compromised. The key to stability was in the original craftsmanship which ensured that every panel and component had been engineered to the finest standard.

Fitment of the doors was all-important: not only did they have to be secure but also water- and draught-proof. Being frameless, this was all the more difficult to achieve. It was also necessary to eliminate any risk of the glass shattering, even if the door was slammed.

Undoubtedly, the shape of the Karmann Ghia was enhanced by its large and inviting doors, which not only helped to give the car a sporty and well-balanced profile, but - at a full metre in width, and extending almost the length of the roof canopy - also made it appear larger and longer than it actually was. The design of the doors is further evidence of Karmann Ghia's futuristic styling because the curved structure dictated that the glass had also to be curved, which was difficult to do at the time.

Access to the car's interior was particularly easy, even to the small and less-inviting rear bench. Designed from the outset as a 2+2, the provision of the rear seat was intended as no more than a luggage platform, although it could be used on short journeys as an occasional seat for a couple of children.

The finish of the Karmann Ghia, just like its Beetle cousin, had to be as good, if not better, than that which Volkswagen customers had come to expect. The outer edges of panels were rolled using a compressed-air tool. To do this effectively, special jigs were necessary to hold each panel firmly in place. The roof had to be treated just as diligently, the outer panels being held in position relative to the inner section and secured with clamps and jigs. Once welded, the units formed a complete roof section. The front and rear wings, instead of being bolted to the bodyshell as in the case of the Karmann Beetle Cabriolet, were welded to the shell.

The use of a large number of small panels meant that the body design of the Karmann Ghia was one of great complexity. Hidden under the outer shell, a whole patchwork of panels added to the ultimate structure, with each component essential to the overall strength of the body.

Under the bonnet no less than five separate panels made up the front assembly. These comprised inner wings on each side, cabin bulkhead, luggage platform and the spare wheel housing. At the rear of the car the drivetrain was responsible for an even more complex arrangement of internal panels. In supplying the required amount of extra strengthening it was necessary to build-in panels transversely. In this way support was provided for the luggage compartment behind the seats, as well as forming a barrier between the engine compartment and cabin.

Karmann had devised a novel way to hinge the front bonnet hatch and the rear engine compartment lid. To avoid the use of struts and stays, over-centred hinges were fitted which, apart from being neat and unobtrusive, allowed the hatches to remain open without further support.

Once welding had been satisfactorily completed and all irregularities in the seams corrected and smoothed out, the whole body was subjected to a rust inhibiting treatment. The process was very similar to that carried out by Volkswagen at Wolfsburg, and it was a condition of the contract that Karmann had to install a full-sized vat at Osnabrück. The installation was big enough to hold fully submerged complete bodies and was designed with a through-put the same as at Wolfsburg. This measure is further indication of Volkswagen's 'belt and braces' approach to manufacture even though production volume at Osnabrück did not warrant such an elaborate system.

Four coats of paint were applied to the body: firstly, the primer, which was then carefully rubbed down by hand to form a perfect base for subsequent coats. The rubbing down process was repeated after the first coat. The third and final coats of paint were applied manually and only a mirror-finish was good enough.

The final part of the build process was to marry chassis and body together, achieved by bolting the body to the chassis with a rubber seal between the two, making the assembly both air- and water-tight. Chassis and body complete, care of the Karmann Ghia was taken over by the finishing department and it was here that all of the remaining component parts were fitted and wiring and instruments installed. Seats were added, trim put into place and, last but not least, wheels and tyres fitted and the battery installed.

In spite of its individually chic styling and sporting appearance, the Karmann Ghia's forte was not so much performance as elegance. The vehicle was never intended as an out-and-out sports car, yet, for all its mechanical ancestry, the pleasure of driving it was in no way compromised. Once behind the wheel Volkswagen characteristics became all the more apparent, emphasized by the car's spartan and almost lacklustre instrumentation and controls, inherited almost entirely from the Beetle. Surprisingly, the basic instruments did not even include a fuel gauge, just a reserve fuel tap to avoid running out of petrol. The metal fascia was almost pure Beetle, too; two dials, random switches and an optional - at a cost - radio was all that greeted the driver. Even the grab handle on top of the dashboard in front of the passenger seat and the lockable glovebox found their way from the Beetle parts bins.

The dashboard arrangement was typical of that found on many European cars of the fifties. An ivory-coloured, two-spoke steering wheel (derived directly from the Beetle) featured the Wolfsburg logo on its centre boss. A speedometer supplemented an identical dial which housed a clock, although prospective owners might have preferred a rev counter, perceived as more in keeping with the car's image.

To the left of the speedometer a pull-switch controlled the choke, and this could be identified easily enough as it was directly above the ignition switch and starter. Switches for the lights and windscreen wiper were situated to the right of the clock and a single stalk, positioned on the left hand side of the steering column, operated the direction indicators. The headlamp dip-switch was particularly awkward to locate; its position to the left of the clutch pedal meant it almost always evaded the driver's searching foot.

Ventilation was soon found to be a problem for Karmann Ghia owners as the heater vents seemed to disperse only warm air which, in the winter, was often not warm enough. Although an air mixer was provided on the central tunnel, the system was typical of cars with air-cooled engines and was largely ineffective. The rear quarterlights were fixed and the only way of ventilating the car was by lowering the windows, which, apart from creating excessive noise, led to some uncomfortable buffeting. The question of ventilation came in for some criticism from *Road & Track* magazine, and reading the road test report one could almost hear the groans of despair at the tester's 'chronic discomfort'. The late John Bolster, who had praised the shape and concept of the car, questioned the lack of a fuel gauge, an omission which irritated him greatly. In all other respects, though, the finish of the car won his approval.

On the question of comfort the Karmann Ghia was beyond reproach. The seats - wider and more relaxing than the Beetle's - had virtually acres of adjustment and could be positioned for height, leg reach and rake. Compared to the Beetle the Karmann Ghia offered almost 6 inches (150mm) of extra cabin width and the seats were trimmed in cloth as standard, although vinyl was optional. To facilitate easy access to the rear, the front seat squabs folded forward and the foam-covered rear bench could be laid flat to provide an ample luggage platform. Alternatively, in the upright position, the seat allowed limited comfort for a couple of children at a pinch, whilst still providing a relatively capacious parcel compartment behind.

19

Elegance aplenty, but modest performance dictated that the Karmann Ghia was often marketed with women in mind. This is a late model car. (Courtesy National Motor Museum)

Although sales of the Karmann Ghia were initially slow, 500 cars had left the factory by the end of 1955. A year later, 10,000 had been built. (Courtesy National Motor Museum)

In the rear, bench-type jump seat cushioned with foam rubber; storage compartment and deep, full-width parcel tray behind backrest.

Wide doors—fitted with big pockets—provide easy entry and exit. The two upholstered "bucket-type" front seats are independently adjustable.

Preparing for launch
The Karmann Ghia went into production during the early part of the summer of 1955. It was the intention that the car should be launched three weeks before the Frankfurt show, which had been scheduled to open on September 19th. As the Coupé went into production at Osnabrück, the Karmann team was devastated at the death, in June 1955, of Dr Karl Feuereisen, one of the leading figures at Wolfsburg, who had been directly involved with the car throughout its development period.

Heinz Nordhoff had already collaborated with Wilhelm Karmann, Luigi Segre and Charles Ladouche to set the Karmann Ghia's launch date for August 27th, but circumstances were to dictate otherwise. It was soon apparent that there was little capacity for storing the new cars at the Osnabrück factory because the DKW was still in production. Realising there was little possibility of finding suitable alternative storage space, the launch date had to be revised to relieve the situation. By bringing the date forward, finished vehicles could be despatched directly to dealers and customers.

July 14th 1955 was the date ultimately chosen to launch Karmann's Coupé, which made its initial appearance at the Kasino Hotel, Westfalen, a short distance to the south of Osnabrück. It was an auspicious occasion with media attention focusing upon Ghia's elegant creation and Karmann's craftsmanship. The fact that Volkswagen's badge adorned the car made the event all the more important. Needless to say the Karmann Ghia was well-received; it was a dream car, the French dubbed it a *poupee vivante* - living doll - and John Bolster described it as a 'perfection of proportion that almost takes one's breath away'. It was perhaps a coincidence that the date chosen to launch the Karmann Ghia was Bastille Day, though some took it as acknowledgement of Charles Ladouche's perseverance in the early days which made the venture possible.

In the run-up to the Coupé's launch an official name for the car had not been found. Wilhelm Karmann had tried in vain to form an association with the car's Italian connection and names such as Corona, San Remo and Ascona were all suggested. None seemed appropriate and all failed to capture the essence of the car. One by one, all were rejected until 'Karmann Ghia' was finally suggested by Wilhelm Karmann. The name rolled easily off the tongue, it aptly summed up the car's origins and everyone involved in the selection seemed to be in total agreement. The final job before the car was launched was the design and placing of the now-famous trademark.

Although commonly referred to as the Karmann Ghia, the car, quite correctly, was known as the Volkswagen Karmann Ghia. Without Volkswagen, of course, there would not have been a Karmann Ghia. In approving the design concept it had been agreed that, because Volkswagen would supply the rolling chassis to Karmann, the car would be marketed solely through Volkswagen dealerships, providing an alternative to the Beetle, Transporter and Karmann Cabriolet, all of which sported the familiar circle embodying the VW emblem. The Volkswagen logo therefore graced the nose of the Karmann Ghia, immediately below the front hatch cover. A further badge, incorporating the Karmann trademark and Ghia's shield, could be found on the front right-hand wing, while the distinctive Karmann Ghia script adorned the engine cover.

The Karmann Ghia, as history has shown, was warmly and enthusiastically received, even though it was an expensive car at DM7500. Such was its popularity that orders soon outstripped production. Between the car's July launch date and the Frankfurt show, however, sales were a trifle slow, with something like 40 cars only being sent to Volkswagen dealers. After the show it was a different story; some 500 cars had been produced by the end of 1955 and a year later something in the order of 10,000 cars had been built.

The launch of the Karmann Ghia prompted speculation that Volkswagen was about to facelift or even completely replace the Beetle. Such conjecture is understandable, especially as the Beetle had been in production since 1945 and in ten years had accounted for the production of over 1 million cars, which included Karmann's Beetle Cabriolet. The question arose of whether the Karmann Ghia was an indication of the shape of things to come?

History has proved, of course, that the Beetle did survive in its near original form, but that is another story. As for performance, the sleek shape of the Karmann Ghia was an indication of the car's athleticism compared to that of its Beetle stablemate. Whereas the 1192cc-engined Beetle claimed a maximum speed of almost 63mph (100.8km/h), the Karmann Ghia managed 77mph (123.2km/h), knocking some 5 seconds off the 0-50mph (0-80km/h) acceleration time in the process. There was a price to pay, however, for

At its launch the Karmann Ghia was priced at about the same level as a Triumph TR. Here, a post-1957 Convertible poses alongside a Triumph. Note the consecutive number plates! (Courtesy Martin McGarry)

improved performance - poorer fuel consumption. Compared to the Beetle's overall 34.5mpg (12lts/100km), the Karmann Ghia achieved only 31.2mpg (13.7lts/100km). Comparing fuel consumption figures with the Beetle is academic; the Karmann Ghia, with its distinct style and selective appeal, was intended for a market in which Porsche, Alfa Romeo, BMW and specialist producers all vied for a share.

The recipe that Volkswagen, Karmann and Ghia devised to produce their sporting car was wholly unique. Others offered merely an off-the-peg, sportingly-styled alternative to what was essentially a standard production vehicle. Of the more interesting alternatives that were to appear to rival the Karmann Ghia was Borgward's Isabella TS Coupé, with surprisingly similar styling; from France, Renault offered the pretty, rear-engined Floride which was eventually superseded by the Caravelle, whilst Simca produced the Plein Ciel and Oceane, both of which were sporting clones of the Aronde Saloon. Skoda enjoyed limited success with its 4-seat drophead Felicia, also rear-engined, but production spanned only 6 years from 1958 to 1964. Volvo's P1800 2-seater Coupé was also a contender for a share of the Karmann Ghia's marketplace, but was considerably more powerful with its 2-litre engine. An unlikely competitor came from Japan in the early '60s with Hino showing-off its rear-engined sports Coupé styled in Italy by Michelotti.

At around £500 on top of the £717 needed to buy the export Beetle, the price of the Karmann Ghia reflected its specialist appeal. The price difference alone was virtually enough to buy either an Austin A30 or a Standard Eight. As for relevant sporting cars, the same amount of money asked for the Karmann Ghia could buy a Triumph TR3, MGA Coupé or the Austin-Healey 100 Six; Sunbeam's Rapier and the MG Magnette were in the running, too. It is a matter of some curiosity, therefore, that *The Motor,* in July 1955 suggested, when it broke the news of the coachbuilt Coupé, that the price was about £630 - approximately half its eventual sales tag figure.

Despite the high price the success of the Karmann Ghia seemed assured from the outset. The American market saw the car as being closer to its own ideas on style; this, at a time when interest in some British sporting models was beginning to wane. John Bolster, writing in *Autosport,* claimed it was one of the most beautiful cars ever built. *Road & Track* magazine wondered whether the enhanced price tag of the Karmann Ghia was worth it for the body alone, considering the relatively small power increase over that of the Volkswagen sedan, and concluded that it probably was.

The Karmann Ghia was not only intended for the European market: America was the all-important goal. Although all 1282 cars sold in 1955 - the first year of production - were destined for Europe, 1956 followed a different trend with 2452 cars out of the 11,556 built exported to the USA. America was already a lucrative market for Volkswagen and, for that matter, Karmann. In 1955 32,662 Beetles found their way across the Atlantic, 1734 of them Karmann Cabriolets. America's share of the Beetle Cabriolet for that year, however, amounted to some 27 per cent of Osnabrück's output.

Early Karmann Ghia sales literature followed a similar style to that for the Beetle Cabriolet and showed the car with exaggerated lines and curves. Brochures of this style, illustrated by Reuters, incorporated the Karmann emblem only, which suggests pre-production publicity. Later brochures were to display the familiar circular Volkswagen logo.

Extending the range

Although the chronology of the Karmann Ghia will be properly discussed in detail in the following chapter, it is interesting to outline development of the range.

Designated Type 143, the original Type 1 Coupé was joined by Type 144, the model notation given to the right-hand drive version. This was introduced in August 1959, the same time as the Type 142, the right-hand drive edition of the Karmann Ghia Convertible, a drophead variant of the Type 1 Coupé. The left-hand drive Convertible had been introduced in August 1957, having let the Coupé initially test the market as a sales barometer.

The success of the Coupé was all that Wilhelm Karmann needed in order to produce a convertible version of Ghia's design. Whereas it had taken five years from the first discussions with Luigi Segre to launch the Coupé, the Convertible was produced at almost breakneck speed. The Convertible appeared only three years after a prototype model had been unveiled and, even at that stage, there was every indication that the car would be a success.

The Karmann Ghia Convertible had just as much verve and chic style as the Coupé but with the added advantage of providing true open-air

Coupé meets Convertible. Frontal styling differences between early and later cars are evident. (Courtesy Martin McGarry)

motoring. It was especially popular in America where a little over 70 per cent of all production was exported.

The body of the Convertible was produced in similar fashion to that of the Coupé, again using the export Beetle chassis in modified form as its base. Karmann's experience had been long established in building Cabriolet bodies and the company had little difficulty producing a folding-top version of the Coupé.

Modifications to the body structure - which consisted of re-inforcements to the sills - were necessary in order to compensate for the loss of rigidity caused by removal of the roof. There were penalties in overall weight, performance and cost, but these factors seemed to little deter would-be purchasers and the car was greeted with infectious enthusiasm.

Karmann had, as has already been illustrated, originally favoured the concept of a convertible sporting Beetle variant. Such was Wilhelm Karmann's eagerness to produce the Ghia-originated convertible that he had a prototype built at Osnabrück as early as 1954. Evidence of the styling progress of the Coupé can be detected from detail development of the Convertible prototype; bumpers were full-width and indicators had been positioned below the headlamps; windscreen wipers had been moved to their definitive position. Most noticeably, the nose was still without its 'nostrils'.

With the hood in raised or lowered position, the Convertible was equally attractive, but for the devoted enthusiast there was only one way to drive this car!

An interesting variation appeared in 1956 when Karmann showed a convertible with a removable hard top. Karmann, however, must have had second thoughts and the car never got beyond the prototype stage.

Various prototypes and variations appeared and disappeared from time to time. Ghia had specific ideas for the future, however, and these manifested themselves as the Type 34 Karmann Ghia. The design, which was popularly referred to as the Type 3 Karmann Ghia, after the VW Type 3, was radical and retained only limited resemblance to the Type 1 Coupé. The Type 3 was not a success and was never produced in convertible form, although a couple of prototypes were built, one of which has survived and is currently on show at Karmann's museum at Osnabrück.

The size and shape of the frontal air intakes identify this car as being one of the first Coupés to receive revised styling. (Courtesy Martin McGarry)

KARMANN Ghia

2
EVOLUTION

By the time the Karmann Ghia appeared, the Beetle was already very well established in both the home market and abroad. The Volkswagen name, by the mid-fifties, had become synonymous with mass-production motoring at its best; the sight, therefore, of an elegant sports coupé or convertible proudly sporting the prominent and instantly recognizable VW logo not only drew attention but also generated respect for the marque.

In 1955 over 279,000 Beetles were produced; a year later the figure was almost exactly a third of a million and rising. Against this background the Karmann Ghia couldn't fail to make anything other than a dramatic debut, which it did at its launch at Westfalen. The scene was repeated at the Frankfurt Show a few weeks later when European motorists could see the car for themselves and understand press enthusiasm.

Karmann's name, to those Beetle owners who had opted for the fashionable and even glamorous drophead variant, was as familiar as the VW emblem on the top of the bonnet. The Karmann Cabriolet was first shown to the car-buying public on 1st July 1949 and, six years later, another Karmann - with an exciting new shape - was offered to a motoring public clamouring for more of the same basic recipe. Importantly, the Karmann Ghia was not intended in any way to take over from the Beetle-shaped Cabriolet, but to complement it as an alternative leisure car in its own right.

For all its aerodynamic styling - as good as anything the Italian carrozzeria could tempt the adventurous and sophisticated motorist with - and better than almost any other volume car producer could offer, the Karmann Ghia was not a performance machine, and neither did it attempt to be: it was good to look at, good to drive and the motorist, generally, was impressed.

Wilhelm Karmann knew his market and was confident of success but still, curiously, felt the need to virtually overstate the car's qualities in early promotional material. Sales brochures told how the product looked like a luxury car but cost far less; how it drove like a sports car but was far more comfortable, and how it was as reliable as any other Volkswagen but was far more attractive.

The Karmann Ghia was eminently suited to Germany's roads; autobahns had been a feature of motoring life since pre-war days and the car's proven Beetle engine was virtually unburstable, being designed to provide long-distance travel at full power. Whereas the Beetle could sustain all-day driving at 100km/h (62mph), the Karmann Ghia, with its higher gearing and streamlined shape, could manage 120km/h (76mph), even with the handicap of an extra 80kg (176lbs) of weight and 2.75in (70mm) overall length.

Generally, the average German motorist of the period had little chance of buying a genuine sports car. Those motorists who could, though, found such vehicles either very expensive or in desperately short supply. It was with some speed, therefore, that the Karmann Ghia built a reputation for itself and found a particular niche, not only in its German home market, but throughout Europe. The American market was also a major factor and if the Beetle Saloon and its sister-car, the Karmann Cabriolet, were anything to go by, the Karmann Ghia had every

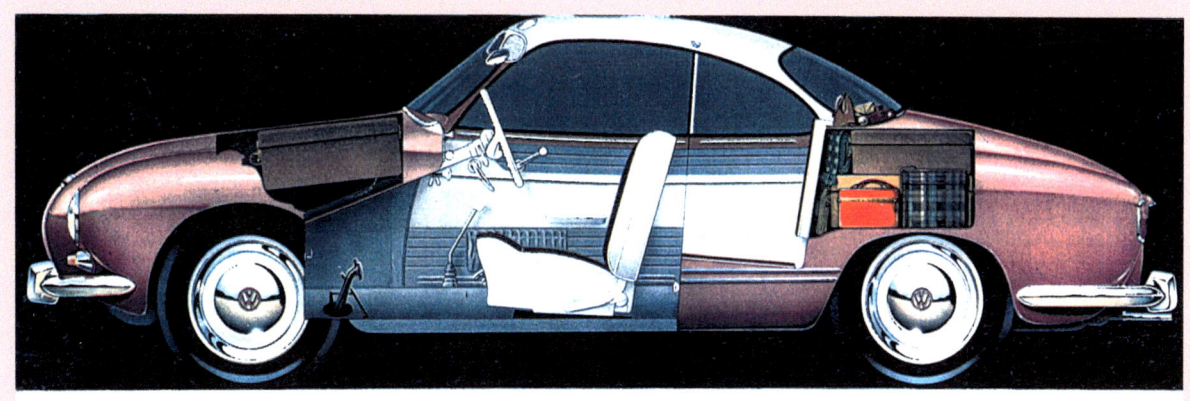

The sporty, form-fitting seats can be adjusted while driving. They rest on metal runners and can be pushed backward or forward – and thereby automatically lower or higher – just at the touch of a lever. Since the seat-backs can also be easily adjusted to three different positions complete driving comfort is assured. Both hoods are lockable from inside the car.

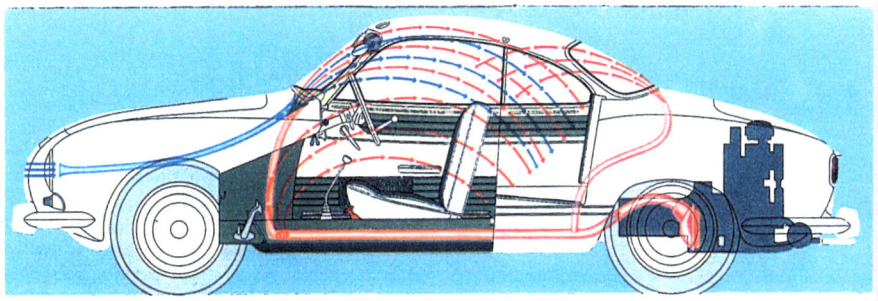

No luggage worries! The luggage space behind the rear seat is surprisingly large and can be doubled simply by folding down the seat back. Now you have ample room to store away all you need for your holiday. There is even more storage space under the front hood.

The standard heating soon has the interior of the car nicely warmed through, the fresh air ventilation ensures the ideal driving temperature. The warm air entering through the four heating ducts at the front and the defroster vent at the rear of the car can be tempered with cool air even when the windows are closed. The cool air can be restricted, as required, to the left or the right hand side only.

Its performance may not have been sporting, but the Karman Ghia's profile certainly was! (Courtesy National Motor Museum)

chance of being truly successful there, too.

The Karmann Ghia's sporting image was so convincing that it took some time to get used to its modest performance. John Bolster, reviewing the car for *Autosport*, was frankly disappointed in its performance about town and saw the lack of acceleration as a serious concern. There was a noticeable change of attitude when the car was unleashed on unrestricted roads, however; from suburban lethargy the car, once released from its shackles, could easily maintain good performance, making it ideal for comfortable, high-speed and long-distance touring.

Having been available on the home market since late summer 1955, exports of the Karmann Ghia to America commenced in 1956 and, by the end of the year, some 2452 cars - 21 per cent of the total output for 1956 - had entered the country. This total was in excess of the number of Karmann Beetle Cabriolets shipped to America in 1956, a trend which continued throughout the Karmann Ghia's production span. The price at point of entry had been set at $2395.

Volkswagen had not always enjoyed the success in the United Sates it saw in the mid-fifties; for the first couple of years or so after production had commenced at Wolfsburg, it was almost impossible to get Americans to buy a Beetle. The situation changed considerably after June 1955 when Volkswagen of America was inaugurated; the rush to sell Beetles virtually eclipsed the arrival of the Karmann Ghia.

The first Karmann Ghia road test for the American motorist was carried out by *Road & Track* magazine in April 1956. Apart from calling the car the Ghia Karmann, the article suggested the vehicle was something of a feeler gauge, intended to test public opinion for the future styling of the Volkswagen Saloon. A significant point about the American Volkswagen scene in the mid-fifties is that there was a complete absence of any marketing strategy; the arrival of the Karmann Ghia, not only in America but also Germany, went by almost unnoticed.

Volkswagen of America likened the Karmann Ghia to the Ford Thunderbird and the Chevrolet Corvette, which appears to be a slightly curious parallel on both accounts. Dubbed "America's only true sports car", the 1956 Corvette was available with a mighty V-8 engine and went on to outsell the Karmann Ghia in both Coupé and Convertible versions every year except 1970 and 1971. By the same token, Ford's Thunderbird was never threatened by the Karmann Ghia.

Interestingly, Volkswagen did recognize its failings in marketing the Karmann Ghia to the American motorist in this way, but not until 1961, six years after the car's Frankfurt debut. "This ad is six years late" claimed the first advert to nationally advertise the Karmann Ghia in America. It explained how the car had mystified millions over the preceding years and how it had been mistaken for an Alfa Romeo or even a Ferrari ... However, for all its lack of promotion in America the Karmann Ghia in both versions nevertheless managed to attract in excess of 38,000 customers.

First modifications
When first launched, the Karmann Ghia was available in a range of just five colour options: Black, Deep Brown, Dark Green, Trout Blue and Gazelle Beige. As sales increased so, too, did the choice of body colours; by 1972, the final year of production, it was possible to select from at least 13 different colour schemes.

Modifications to the Coupé, Types 143 and 144 and, subsequently the Convertible, Types 141 and 142, emanated from two sources, Wolfsburg and Osnabrück. Mechanical and chassis improvements, created by Volkswagen for the Beetle, were generally incorporated within the Karmann Ghia; Karmann, naturally, introduced certain modifications of its own, apart from interior and body styling, and some of these eventually found their way to the Beetle. An example of this is that the Karmann Ghia was specified with tubeless tyres from the outset, yet these were not fitted on the Volkswagen Beetle as standard until July 1956.

Some confusion has arisen about modification dates and model years. Until 1955 Volkswagen used the calendar year as a means of identifying the production year, i.e. January to December. After 1955 this method of distinguishing model years was changed to August to August. Not only did the change bring Volkswagen into line with other manufacturers, it also enabled synchronisation of the product year with the company's annual shutdown.

The first major modifications to the Coupé coincided with the arrival of the Convertible in September 1957. After this date, with two models in production, modifications in general terms applied equally to both cars, although special attention was given to one or the other car where body styling dictated.

Karmann Ghia owners' exasperation at having to constantly guess the amount of fuel remaining in the tank, as well as being almost totally at the mercy of the tank's reserve tap, resulted in a circular fuel gauge being fitted to the dashboard between the clock and the speedometer. A dipstick in the petrol tank did previously provide a guide to how much fuel remained, but the process of checking the tank's contents was quite inconvenient. Having a dipstick as a fuel gauge was by no means unusual at the time and the writer remembers having to check the fuel dipstick in a fifties Citroën 2CV. The petrol reserve tap on the Karmann Ghia was still fitted, however, which was typical of Wolfsburg's belt-and-braces policy. Some of the early Karmann Ghias could be found with makeshift perpendicular gauges which had been fitted by their owners.

The lack of a fuel gauge on early Beetles and Karmann Ghias did prompt the appearance of a manually-operated accessory petrol gauge; made by Drager with Volkswagen in mind, the device - which included a plastic tube that led to the fuel tank - could be manually pumped and the needle on the dial recorded the volume of fuel remaining. An official 'add-on' electric gauge was made by VDO and was available for late fifties Beetles.

A number of minor, but nevertheless important, mechanical changes were introduced between the time the Coupé was launched and the Convertible made its debut. Not only did Volkswagen decide upon the use of SAE 80 transmission oil, instead of the SAE 90 as previously specified, a re-designed oil cooler was fitted and the oil pump was beefed-up. The timing gear was also respecified and aluminium alloy used in its manufacture instead of Resitex. The pressure required to operate the clutch pedal was considered too great and, by redesigning the thrust spring assembly, this was reduced from 6kg (13.2lbs) to just 1kg (2.2lbs).

As well as the provision of a fuel gauge, a number of other modifications were specified from 1957, including better sound insulation, more powerful braking, increased cabin comfort and safety measures. These were all improvements which trial and error -

and customer feedback - had deemed appropriate.

The provision of a layer of sound-deadening material, some 12mm (0.5in) thick, against the bulkhead between the cabin and the engine compartment, successfully reduced the noise level from the drivetrain. Stopping power was effectively improved by increasing the width of the brake shoes. For driver comfort, the design of the accelerator pedal was changed from the roller-ball type found on the Beetle to an organ-pedal device. At the same time the car was fitted with a new type of steering wheel which, although retaining its two spokes, was dished in shape and incorporated a semi-circular horn push. Interior trimming of the car underwent minor changes and door trims were covered in vinyl instead of cloth and vinyl as previously. Armrests and chrome embellishments were also added, as was a larger rear-view mirror.

The Convertible arrives

Overall, the Type 1 Convertible, Karmann Ghia Types 141 and 142 (left- and right-hand drive respectively), was very much a low-volume car compared to the Type 143 and 144 (again, left- and right-hand drive respectively) Coupé. The Karmann Ghia Convertible enjoyed considerable exclusivity; it was built in such small numbers that it did not even achieve 1 per cent of the Beetle Saloon's output. Put into production at Osnabrück on 1st August 1957, the Convertible was unveiled at the Frankfurt Motor Show the following month, where it was seen as an exciting alternative to the already much admired Karmann Ghia Coupé. Like its Coupé sister, the Convertible was modelled upon the export 1200 Volkswagen chassis with standard Beetle running gear. None of the extrovertly chic styling first seen on the Coupé was lost, and the new Convertible presented a unique and formidable challenge to some of the more prestigious sports tourers then available.

The Karmann Ghia Convertible was eminently suited to Karmann's production process, which had traditionally constructed fine Cabriolet bodies. The company's experience had allowed the Convertible to be produced without any further styling input from Carrozzeria Ghia; the design changes needed to convert the original Coupé concept were all carried out in-house and the car was identical to its sister as high as the waist line. Structurally, the Convertible necessitated substantial reinforcement to account for the loss of torsional strength caused by the absence of the steel roof. In order to retain the smooth and unrestricted line of the bodywork, with its wide doors and frameless windows, considerable bracing supports, which were drilled in order to reduce weight without compromising strength, were added to the sills. It was necessary also to apply extra strengthening around the rear of the cabin, especially in the area where the hood, when in the lowered position, could be easily and safely stowed away.

Even though every conceivable measure was taken to reduce the weight of the reinforcing material the Convertible was, nevertheless, considerably heavier than the Coupé. The increased weight resulted in diminished performance which shaved 2mph (3.2km/h) off the car's top speed. Fuel consumption was also adversely affected but the charms of the car overcame any customer dissatisfaction in this respect.

The suggestion that the Coupé be supplied with a removable roof had been vetoed. Now, the arrival of the Convertible gave the Karmann Ghia buyer a definite choice of cars. With regard to aesthetics, both cars were supremely good-looking and the Convertible, with its hood in the raised position, offered just as much comfort as the Coupé: the hood itself was nothing less than a work of art, taking a couple of craftsmen at least four hours to construct. As is to be expected from a company with Karmann's reputation, the hood was made from the finest materials, and the finish was far beyond that found on many production sports cars. Three layers of materials were used in the hood's manufacture; the outer skin was formed from mohair and the headlining from woolcloth. Sandwiched between the headlining and the outer skin, horsehair provided effective insulation. The fit of the hood was such that it was both completely waterproof and draught-free and extremely easy to raise and lower. It could not have been simpler to operate; once raised and secured into two catches above the windscreen surround, it could then be locked into position by the turn of a handle. When lowered, the hood could be fastened down with a cover press-studded into place.

A disadvantage of the Convertible compared to the Coupé was that, when lowered, the hood folded, albeit very neatly, into the luggage compartment behind the rear occasional seat which, obviously, restricted luggage space. The hood on the convertible had a rear window made from plastic, unlike that found on the Beetle Cabriolet which used glass. The rear window was also

Something like 40 per cent of all Karmann Ghia production was destined for the USA. Note the American specification bumpers on this Convertible; it also appears to have rear indicator repeaters. (Courtesy National Motor Museum)

smaller than the Coupé's which was rather a disadvantage as it impaired visibility; a further problem was that the plastic window was easily scratched and was, of course, a security risk.

For those motorists who clamoured for open-air motoring but wanted the protection the Coupé offered, it was possible to have a Coupé fitted with a sun roof. The Golde sliding steel roof could be specified as a cost option, although this accessory was rarely fitted.

The Convertible was available in a different range of colours to that of the Coupé, although Black was standard for both models. Until July 1959, as well as Black the colour options were Pearl White, Diamond Grey, Cardinal Red, Amazon (green), Graphite Silver and Bernina (blue).

Not only was the Convertible heavier and slightly slower than the Coupé, it was also more expensive. At DM8250, the Convertible went on sale with a DM750 price disadvantage but, for all that, it attracted many potential customers. It did, however, put the car into the price league of some of the British speciality sports cars such as Daimler's SP250 and the Austin Healey 3000.

If the Karmann Ghia looked as if it should be a rapid car, the lack of scorching performance, ironically, added to its charm. Both Volkswagen and Karmann made no secret of the Karmann Ghia's sedateness; instead, Volkswagen latched onto this particular aspect and customers appreciated Wolfsburg's down-to-earth honesty.

Often considered a poor relation to the Porsche, the Karmann Ghia never pretended to be anything other than what it was. Neither did it try to emulate the Porsche or, for that matter, any other full-blooded sports car. When all's said and done, though, it was an attractive hand-built car, the production of which was necessarily limited. Furthermore, it used a reliable chassis with which there was little to compare or compete.

Further changes

Changes to mechanical specification were generally applied to the Coupé and

American specification bumpers are a feature of this Convertible. The re-styled front was effective from August 1959. (Courtesy National Motor Museum)

Convertible at the same time except, naturally, where the modifications were restricted to those areas specific to one or other model. The most significant styling changes were, in the main, cosmetic and were made in August 1959 for the 1960 model year.

Before the alterations in styling are described in detail, it is necessary to identify mechanical improvements instigated by Volkswagen during 1958 and up to the end of the 1959 model year, which ended in August. The carburettor underwent some modification with a re-designed idling screw and a nylon venturi in place of aluminium alloy. The kingpin washers were formed from plastic instead of fibre, and the oil drain plug was replaced with a magnetic type.

August 1959 is significant in Karmann Ghia chronology due to the car's styling facelift. The revised cosmetic treatment coincided with the introduction of right-hand drive versions of both Coupé and Convertible models, designed primarily for the British and Swedish markets. The shape of the front wings was altered so that they were less curved at the leading edge. The result had a double effect: firstly, the line of the wing was smoothed out and, secondly, the headlamps were positioned 2 inches (50mm) higher. The reason for raising the headlamps was in order to meet international standards. The bumpers were also repositioned, but the most noticeable change was to the 'nostrils' on the front panels which allowed fresh air to enter the car. These were altered in shape and made larger, following the contours of the nose assembly. Whereas the nostrils were previously embellished with just two chrome strips, a grille with three horizontal bars now added to the brightwork. At the rear of the car the light clusters were enlarged and made oval shaped, which blended with the car's curvaceous body line.

There were changes inside the car, too. The reserve tap for the petrol supply was deemed no longer necessary. As a safety feature, as well as an essential driving aide, windscreen washers were specified. To answer the criticism of

The type of front turn indicators and the flat ventilated wheel trims distinguish this as a post-1966 Convertible. (Courtesy Martin McGarry)

a lack of ventilation in the Coupé, the rear side windows were hinged to enable them to be opened slightly. Mechanically, a hydraulic steering damper was fitted which assisted in suppressing much of the road shock felt through the steering wheel.

These styling changes had been conceived as early as 1957 and a prototype car was built which incorporated some of the ideas then being considered. In addition to the rear-opening windows, a plan was proposed to install quarterlights in the front windows, which did not particularly enhance the profile of the car. Possibly the most striking alteration was to the rear lights which looked very odd. Not surprisingly, these two proposals were rejected.

More power
Whilst minor modifications continued to the Beetle-orientated running gear, the first significant change to the power unit since the beginning of Karmann Ghia production was implemented for the 1961 model year. A new engine was made available for the Karmann Ghia at the same time as it was fitted to the Beetle and, although cubic capacity remained unchanged at 1192cc, output increased from 30bhp to 34bhp. The compression ratio also increased from 6.6:1 to 7.0:1. Not content with introducing a new engine, revisions were also carried out to produce a modified gearbox.

The new engine arrived at a time when sales of Volkswagens were breaking all records. During 1961 alone, over 0.75 million cars were produced at Wolfsburg. Volkswagens were also being built in Brazil in addition to the Karmann products at Osnabrück, and total production worldwide for 1961 amounted to approximately 860,000 cars. There is no doubt that the 30bhp engine had worked well and had, up to the time of the new engine's introduction, been fitted in over 3.5 million Volkswagens worldwide.

Volkswagen had introduced the 34bhp engine in May 1959 when it was first fitted to the Type 2 Volkswagen - the Transporter. An important point about this engine is that very few of the components are common to the previous unit. This obviously has to been taken into account and calls for special care, when undertaking overhauls, engine rebuilds and restoration projects.

Apart from the welcome increase in power, an advantage of the 34bhp engine was that it was appreciably quieter than its predecessor. This was achieved, in the main, by decreasing the cooling fan speed, made possible by re-designing the crankshaft pulley, reducing it in size and modifying the dynamo pulley to increase its size. The dynamo pedestal was also modified and, instead of being cast into the crankcase, was designed to be detachable.

Tappet clearances on both inlet and exhaust valves were altered from 0.004in to 0.008in; a more durable crankshaft with larger bearings was fitted within a strengthened crankcase. New cylinder heads were designed which incorporated re-shaped combustion chambers that allowed the valves to sit at an angle; by spacing the cylinder heads further apart, it was possible to improve engine cooling.

Changes were also made to the carburettor and the Solex 28 PICT unit was specified in place of the Solex 28 PCI. Most significant about this modification was that the new carburettor was equipped with an automatic choke. A problem had previously existed with carburettor icing in winter; modifying the air cleaner so that it fed warm air to the carburettor in cold weather went some way toward preventing further difficulties. In striving to improve cold weather starting, the left-hand heat exchanger was modified to allow warm air to permeate the air cleaner which sat on top of the carburettor.

The new gearbox also improved the Karmann Ghia's performance. Synchromesh was added to the bottom ratio and the gearbox casing made to resemble that used on the Porsche 356. It was constructed with a single casing instead of being split into two separate halves as previously. Gear ratios were revised to provide optimum performance and a modified top gear ratio - altered from 0.82:1 to 0.89:1 - ensured a top speed of 125km/h

Most significant of the styling changes from August 1959 were larger 'nostrils' and a higher front wing line. (Courtesy National Motor Museum)

(77.5mph). An obvious advantage of the new gearbox was its greater accessibility and easier servicing; larger bearings enabled the axle tubes to be removed without having to entirely dismantle the gearbox as before.

Fuel consumption, as a result of the increased power, suffered to a certain degree, and the overall figure dropped from 35.2mpg (8 Lts/100km) to 31.2mpg (9 Lts/100km). Trials with the Karmann Ghia on the test track revealed that maintaining top

In addition to the larger nostrils and higher wing profile, the Karmann Ghia lost its 'cigar-shape', a term often used to describe earlier cars. (Courtesy National Motor Museum)

68 COJ was the subject of a nut-and bolt-restoration by Karmann Ghia enthusiast Richard Hobson. The car was built in 1960 and has the 34bhp engine. As a surviving RHD model it is somewhat rare.
(Courtesy Martin McGarry)

speed increased fuel consumption to a little under 28mpg (10 Lts/100km) but more leisurely driving provided an economical 40-44mpg (10.5-9.5 Lts/100km).

Improvements had been made to the Karmann Ghia's heating and ventilation system and criticisms levelled at this aspect of the car soon

An exciting car called for exciting publicity material. This brochure has an American flavour.
(Courtesy National Motor Museum)

The Volkswagen Karmann Ghia. Beauty plus Sense. Surely it's sensible to treat yourself to economy. And economy you get – whether your desire runs to either Coupé or Convertible. The spirited Volkswagen engine is capable of turning up a cruising speed of 71 m.p.h. – yet it can be run at full throttle for miles and miles and still deliver unparalleled fuel economy. It's fun to drive a VW Karmann Ghia. It's fun to get all those miles to a gallon, too!

The large, velour-trimmed area in the rear is another feature of the VW Karmann Ghia. And most practical, too. The foam-rubber upholstered bench serves as storage space or can seat two additional passengers on occasion!

Very neat. A flick of the wrist and the rear storage space is doubled in size! And there's more room for additional luggage under the front bonnet. Coupé or Convertible, every bit of space is sensibly put to good use.

Poor ventilation was always the Karmann Ghia's weakness. In this publicity brochure special mention is made of the vent intended to de-mist the rear window. (Courtesy National Motor Museum)

after launch had largely ceased when *The Autocar* tested the car again in April 1961. There were but few major concerns about the car, the most serious being the positioning of the pedals and the headlamp dip-switch. Compliments far outweighed criticism, however, and the car was recognised as the well-equipped and exclusive tourer it was.

The next milestone in Type 1 chronology involves a further increase in power, which came about from August 1965 for the 1966 model year. This was but a short-term measure as, a year later, a far more drastic development occurred which resulted in a major change to the Karmann Ghia's engine capacity.

Between the previous increase in power and that of August 1965, the Type 1 cars bravely soldiered on without any major design alteration. What modifications there were consisted mainly of mechanical changes common to both Karmann Ghia and Beetle specifications. During these four years, however, certain improvements were aimed at increasing comfort and safety. The design of the heating and ventilation controls was altered to allow more efficient operation: independent levers to adjust the amount of heat and air - one to the front of the car and the other to the rear - replaced the single rotary valve previously fitted. Both levers, one red (for the front), the other white (for the rear) were positioned each side of the gearchange lever but, prior to this, the rotary knob had been positioned to the right of the gearshift. Seat belts, which were by this time considered a necessity, were catered for and anchorage points installed. Curiously for a car such as this, the belts themselves were not supplied and had to be ordered separately as an accessory item.

An overtaking mirror was installed on the front off-side wing, although this

American specification Karmann Ghias had to have different bumpers to those cars destined for Britain and Europe. These bumpers - which were intended to give greater protection when parking - are often popular with owners of European specification cars. Note the white hood, always a favourite choice with American owners. (Courtesy Martin McGarry)

was later moved to the driver's door. A new interior mirror was fitted, which was encompassed within a chrome surround, and sun visors were made to swivel in an arc to give side protection instead of merely providing up and down adjustment. The steering wheel was re-designed with a semi-circular horn-push which replaced the thumb pushes built into the two wheel spokes. In a further attempt to provide greater driving comfort, extra sound-proofing was installed to deaden engine noise.

A number of modifications were implemented to keep abreast of the Beetle's technical developments, and these included a design alteration to the clutch lever and plate, tie rods - which were made to be adjustable and free from maintenance - and new rear wheel bearings.

At Wolfsburg, developments in model structure looked as if they might force the Karmann Ghia in a new direction. The Type 3 Karmann Ghia had appeared and it was initially intended, possibly, to supersede the Type 1. However, progressive changes to the Type 1's specification ensured the car would remain in existence. There were, nevertheless, serious deficiencies in respect of the car's performance capability and these led to the power increase for the 1966 model year, which is discussed later in this chapter.

Although not part of Karmann Ghia chronology, it is a point of interest that chassis modifications applied to the Karmann Ghia were also used to develop the Volkswagen Type 147, a small van of delightful proportions and quite unlike anything else Volkswagen produced, including the Type 2 Transporter. Constructed by Westfalia, which is better known for camper vans, the Type 147 was unavailable to the general public and was normally reserved for official or utility purposes. Generally used by the German and Swiss Post Office for postal services, Lufthansa also operated a fleet of 147s for airport services.

A new direction - arrival of the Type 3

The prototype development car unveiled in 1957 was but a step in the progression towards re-shaping the Karmann Ghia for the next, and subsequent, decades. A whole host of design proposals were suggested for what was perceived as the spearhead of the Karmann Ghia range of cars, which would take over from the model better known as the Type 1.

Launched in the autumn of 1961 at the Frankfurt Motor Show, the Type 3 Karmann Ghia (which was actually designated the Type 34) made its cautious official debut. Derived from two specific origins, the Type 3 Volkswagen chassis, together with bodywork styled by Carrozzeria Ghia in Turin, the car very quickly assumed the title Type 3 Karmann Ghia. Compared to the classic lines of the Type 1 cars, the Type 3 was totally new and was never really fully appreciated. The reaction from the general public on seeing the new Karmann Ghia was far less enthusiastic than it had been when the Type 1 was introduced. Nevertheless, the Type 3 did then, and does now, have its staunch admirers.

Like the Type 1 cars, the Type 3 had its specific model notation system. Left- and right-hand drive Coupés were designated 343 and 344 respectively but the situation becomes unclear with the appearance of Types 345 and 346. The last two type numbers indicate an electric sunroof as part of the car's original equipment, and confirmed whether the vehicle had left- (345) or right-hand drive (346). Volkswagen's numbering system was intended to positively distinguish between each of the variants; the first digit identifying the chassis type, the second that it was indeed a Karmann Ghia and, thirdly, the precise vehicle type. A right-hand drive Type 3 Coupé with an electric sunroof would, therefore, be a 346, whilst a left-hand drive Type 1 Convertible a 141.

The possibility of updating, remodelling or even completely replacing the Type 1 Coupé and Convertible had been on the minds of Volkswagen, Karmann and Ghia since 1957-8, when a series of designs had begun to emerge from Ghia's studios. From those drawings it is clear that a common theme was beginning to materialise which was later to manifest itself in the definitive car.

The Type 1 Convertible is possibly the most revered of all Karmann Ghias. This car, like many others, was exported to California. (Courtesy Martin McGarry)

'Razor-edge' styling is a Type 3 characteristic. The slim roof and narrow pillars gave the car its sleek appearance. Although attractive, the Type 3 was never as curvaceous as the Type 1. (Courtesy National Motor Museum)

Top: The Type 3 was styled to specifically appeal to American tastes - but was never sold there! (Courtesy National Motor Museum)

Above: Plans were in hand to produce a 4-seater Cabriolet replacement for the Karmann Beetle. Apart from the prototype, however, production went no further due to structural difficulties. Note the neat cooling louvres below the hood. (Courtesy National Motor Museum)

The design of the Type 3 Karmann Ghia was the work of Sergio Sartorelli and the development period was closely related to that of the Type 3 Volkswagen. Sergio Sartorelli, who had studied engineering at the Turin Polytechnic, had been employed by Ghia since 1954, when he joined the Studio's styling department as an assistant. By the end of 1956 Luigi Segre, who had initially appointed Sartorelli, promoted him to directorship of the department. At around the same time a young American, Tom Tjaarda, was put under Sartorelli in order to gain first-hand experience of the European motor industry. Tom Tjaarda already had extensive knowledge of the American car business, his father having been deeply involved with motor car design in the 1930s. John Tjaarda had helped shape the products from Detroit two decades previously

Right: The Volkswagen Type 3, on which the Type 3 Karmann Ghia was based. (Courtesy National Motor Museum)

and was responsible for the infamous Lincoln Zephyr. Tom Tjaarda worked on the Type 3 Karmann Ghia project alongside Sergio Sartorelli, which may explain some of the car's well-defined American styling attributes.

It was not until 1959, at the time of the Geneva Motor Show, that the decision to proceed with an updated Karmann Ghia was taken. Contracts for developing the car were signed by Luigi Segre, on behalf of Ghia, and Wilhelm Karmann; suddenly, mayhem ensued and Luigi Segre demanded from Sergio Sartorelli a number of suitable designs - at a moment's notice. Sartorelli, in fact, had just three days in which to prepare drawings - albeit relatively simple detail drafts - for the new car.

There is little doubt that Sartorelli burned the midnight oil at the Turin studios. Whilst studies had previously been undertaken, Segre's design brief was articulate and Sartorelli had the difficult task of translating what he had been told over the telephone into well defined sketches in keeping with Segre's demands. Sartorelli performed this unenviable task well and rushed the designs to Segre whilst staying at Geneva. Having taken time to study in detail each of Sartorelli's drawings, Luigi Segre took the decision to present just one design, instead of a selection, to Wilhelm Karmann. It appears Karmann was impressed with what he saw and gave the go-ahead for Ghia to proceed with the car's development. The job of actually building the Type 3 Karmann Ghia at Osnabrück went to Karmann's chief body engineer, Johannes Beeskow. Beeskow was well acquainted with the Volkswagen and had been instrumental in producing the Rometsch in 1951.

Timing of the decision to go ahead with the new Karmann Ghia coincided neatly with the Karmann company's involvement with Wolfsburg in an effort to produce what was seen as an eventual replacement for the Volkswagen Beetle Cabriolet. Karmann's role had been to prepare a delectable 4-seater convertible, based upon the design of car that had evolved at Wolfsburg for a brand new Saloon, and which would also have a station wagon-type vehicle as a relative. Importantly, the new Volkswagen would retain the Beetle's principle of a rear-mounted engine and drivetrain.

Germany's economic revival from what was a desperate situation immediately after the Second World War turned into something of a boom in the late 1950s, the surging development of the country's motor industry matching the national trend. It was with some curiosity, therefore, that commentators wondered about Volkswagen's virtual one-model policy. Whilst this can be understood up to a point, it is also possible to appreciate Heinz Nordhoff's policy of letting well alone if all was working smoothly. With the Beetle selling in huge and ever-increasing numbers without there being any sign that customers wanted anything different, why change the design?

Plans for developing a Type 3 Volkswagen were seriously advanced as early as 1957, having been initiated two years earlier. As a replacement for the Type 1 Volkswagen, there was no reason not to have introduced it sooner; each time the issue arose Heinz Nordhoff applied the brakes, letting the Beetle enjoy its miraculous following a while longer. By the time the project was allowed to get under way, Nordhoff saw the Type 3 not as a replacement for the Beetle - sales were far too high to warrant substituting it - but as a separate model in its own right and an alternative to an already truly successful design.

The new model's launch was very much tied in with events current in the German motor industry. The demand for cars, due to an easing of the financial recession, resulted in those companies normally associated with the production of economy cars producing designs which reflected greater affluence. As well as still catering for the economy market (from which there would always be a demand) such companies were able to expand their model ranges to produce larger and more appealing vehicles that could challenge the Beetle, if only in its least expensive form. A similar situation had occurred in Italy where a plethora of inexpensive cars and runabouts, some of which were related more to the motorcycle than a car, had resulted in Fiat introducing its minuscule 500 Nuova to combat competition from Germany in the form of NSU, Lloyd and Goggomobil.

Volkswagen's Type 3 Variant made its debut at the Frankfurt Motor Show in the autumn of 1961; it had far greater carrying capacity than did the Beetle, although the car was built upon exactly the same principles as the original Volkswagen and shared the Beetle's wheelbase dimensions. The shape of the new Volkswagen was completely at odds with the Beetle, the newcomer being very box-like whilst the existing model had not one angular corner and better resembled an egg.

For the Type 3, a wholly new flat-four boxer unit of 1500cc capacity was used. A feature of the 1500cc power

VW 1500 S Sedan

This car offers you even more.

More in exterior elegance through new flashing indicators, chromium-plated rear reflectors, and chromium borders on the sides.

More equipment, such as hinged quarter windows, two parking lights, an electric clock, and a headlamp flasher.

Likewise, a windscreen wiper with speed fully adjustable.

And automatic securing of front seat backrests. Plus rear luggage compartment illumination.

Just a few of the many extras, all at no extra price. (Only the two-tone finish costs more.)

But that's still not all.

The Volkswagen 1500 S, besides being more comfortable and elegant, is also faster. It has an air-cooled, 66 hp twin carburetter engine—85 miles per hour. And maximum speed is cruising speed. You can keep it there all day—if you want to.

The Type 3 Karmann Ghia was designed on the Type 3 Saloon platform. Much more box-like than the Beetle, the Type 3 Saloon sported a lower profile than the original Volkswagen. (Author's collection)

unit was a lower profile which allowed it to be installed in the equally low profile of the Type 3 notchback engine compartment. Similar to the Beetle, the engine of the Type 3 fitted over and aft of the rear axle. Such was the design of both engine and bodyshell that two distinct luggage compartments were provided: at the front, as on the Beetle, and a second, relatively small hatch, above the engine. To get to the engine after lifting the 'boot' lid, it was necessary to lift up an inner panel which also served as the floor of the second luggage compartment. This arrangement for the new generation Volkswagen was entirely convenient and silenced the disparaging remarks about the Beetle's somewhat limited luggage space.

Included in the plans to extend the Type 3 Volkswagen range was a 4-seater Convertible. Heinz Nordhoff had placed the design in the custody of Karmann who, in turn, was careful to follow the overall styling of the Saloon as far as possible. So closely did the Convertible follow the Saloon that it had been possible to use standard panels throughout below the waist line; the hood folded neatly away leaving the profile of the car quite uncluttered and rear seat passenger accommodation was not in any way compromised. Volkswagen saw the car as a potential successor to the Karmann-built Beetle Cabriolet. Two major drawbacks to the 4-seater Convertible were evident: it appeared far too ordinary and perhaps more was expected in terms of styling, especially as it was Karmann who had produced the distinctive Beetle Cabriolet before going on to build the elegant Type 1 Ghia Coupé and Convertible. Secondly, there were structural difficulties with the prototype cars which displayed a fundamental weakness in torsional rigidity. As if these two problems were not enough, public reaction to the car at the 1961 Frankfurt Motor Show was decidedly cool. It did not take Volkswagen long to realise that the 4-seat Convertible would require

The car that never was! The prototype Type 3 Karmann Ghia Convertible would have made a pretty alternative to the Type 3 Karmann Ghia Coupé. So sure was Volkswagen of its success that publicity brochures were prepared for the car's launch. (Courtesy National Motor Museum)

much more time and effort to get the design right ...

With no evidence of sales of either the Beetle Cabriolet or the Karmann Ghia deteriorating, Heinz Nordhoff can probably be excused for making the decision to let the project pass quietly into obscurity. Although a number of prototype cars had been built, the car never went into production.

Luckily, a prototype Karmann-inspired Convertible survives in the Karmann museum at Osnabrück.

At the same time as Heinz Nordhoff contracted Karmann to prepare the 4-seater Variant Convertible, he also instructed Ghia and Karmann to produce Coupé and Convertible versions, also to be based on the Type 3 Volkswagen. There was every intention, it would seem, that the new models would eventually take the place of the Type 1 Karmann Ghia.

From the outset the styling of the Type 3 Karmann Ghia was controversial and, in retrospect, the clear leanings towards American taste can be seen as something of a mistake. The classic styling of the Type 1, so beloved by European markets and even more highly regarded by the American market, had disappeared. As it happened, the Karmann Ghia's American customers were far more appreciative of European styling,

Presentation of the Type 3 Karmann Ghia Convertible. Problems with the body structure prevented the car from going into production. (Courtesy National Motor Museum)

The large window area and huge windscreen of the Karmann Ghia Type 3 is very noticeable in this publicity photograph. (Courtesy National Motor Museum)

preferring it to anything then available in the United States. Had American customers not been so impressed they would have otherwise purchased an American product. The irony of it is that the Type 3 Karmann Ghia was never officially available in the United States, although several cars were sent there for publicity purposes. Early Type 3 brochures are clearly aimed at attracting American customers and cars which have found their way across the Atlantic Ocean have been specially imported by Karmann Ghia enthusiasts.

Most striking of the Type 3's features was the frontal appearance. Hardly any Type 1 characteristics were evident and the familiar 'nostrils' had gone entirely. In place of the soft curvaceousness of the Type 1, Type 3 styling was notably aggressive and forthright, an image accentuated by the distinctive 4-headlamp system. With only a hint of the rounded bullet-shaped nose remaining, frontal styling was made all the more extraordinary by the hooded or 'eyebrow' affect. This impression was given because the swage line was continuous, starting at the doors and continuing along the front of the car, finally plunging down to bumper level. In its prototype forms, (which, incidentally, were greatly akin to the definitive car) the foglamps were positioned somewhat closer to the headlamps in a much more typical 4-lamp arrangement.

Of special interest is the existence, in the museum at Osnabrück, of a prototype car sporting a fastback body. This, too, has four headlamps but, in this case, of a twin-lamp system. The effect of the fastback makes the car seem larger than it actually is and the slightly different frontal styling is less aggressive. The fastback was not peculiar to the prototype car, however, as cars assembled by Karmann in Brazil also incorporated this feature.

There is little doubt that the larger proportions of the Type 3 Karmann Ghia resulted in an extremely well-balanced styling exercise. In what could loosely be described as a 'razor-edged' style, the Type 3 appeared appreciably longer and wider than the Type 1; the increased bonnet length and longer rear boot gave it an is-it-coming-or-going? appearance and added to the car's appeal. Particular features of the model were its narrow pillars and ultra-slim roof line; the razor-edged effect was made all the more significant by the sharply-raked windscreen which extended virtually into the roof, and the vast, deeply-curved rear window.

The side profile was dramatically sleek and elegant, due, in part, to the width of the doors, which were wider by 3 inches (75mm) than those on Type 1 cars.

The Type 3's rear styling was also in direct contrast to that of the Type 1 Coupé and Convertible. The swage line was again responsible, as it continued around the top of the engine compartment having originated just forward of and above the wheelarch. The high sill extended downwards with a valance that housed the rear lamps, whose circular lenses were reminiscent of trans-Atlantic styling. Overall, the shape and style of the Type 3 was remarkably similar to Chevrolet's early Corvair.

Although 5.5 inches (140mm) longer than the Type 1, the Type 3 Karmann Ghia was no wider overall, although it appeared so. It was, in fact, minutely narrower by less than 0.5 of an inch (10mm). The clever body styling, however, allowed greater elbow room inside the car, giving a completely different feel. The Type 3 was closer to the ground than the Type 1; 6.8 inches (172mm) instead of 5.4 inches (138mm), yet the overall height of the

The Karmann Ghia chassis. (Author's collection)

But there's a Volkswagen in every Karmann Ghia. Something that pleases nearly everybody.

Because everybody prefers a car they can rely on. As they can on the Volkswagen. Which is why it is so important that every Karmann Ghia is basically a Volkswagen. As regards chassis. Engine. Workmanship. Concept. Which in its turn means that every Karmann Ghia can be serviced and repaired in any VW dealership. The world over.
You'll find VW service stations everywhere you go — there are 8,754 of them in all. This means you can always get help no matter where you are. (If something should go wrong.) And the help you get is efficient. Because the repairs are carried out by VW trained mechanics and checked by VW trained foremen. They work with special tools — specially developed for VW. And with genuine VW spare parts. Which carry the same guarantee as a new car.
And with VW exchange parts which are up to 50% cheaper because we take the old part in payment. (Whereby individual parts which aren't up to scratch are replaced by brand new ones.) And every repair is carried out at VW prices. Everywhere. Even on the island of St. Maarten in the Carribean. (If you've got good eyes you may just find it on the map.) The home of Dr. Kenneth Brown. Who's the proud owner of a VW workshop.

car was greater by 10mm (0.5 inches). Whilst the wheelbase dimensions were the same on both cars, the Type 3 had a marginally wider - by 1.25 inches (30mm) - front track, and a considerably bigger rear track which accounted for an extra 3.80 inches (96mm).

Inside the car, the Type 3 Karmann Ghia retained the 2+2 seating configuration of the Type 1; the front seats were different in design inasmuch as they were fully adjustable for rake as well as being wider, which was eminently suitable for long-distance travel. Type 1 seats were completely adequate and certainly did not lack in comfort, although they were not as adjustable as the squabs reclined to just three positions. The rear seat on the Type 3 was no less awkward than that of Type 1 cars, although a point in the Type 3's favour was the enhanced headroom made possible by the cabin shape. Ventilation was a little better than previously; opening front quarterlights, together with limited opening of the rear side windows, gave improved airflow. The large glass area gave the car a distinct airiness, but by far the most coveted feature was the Golde electric steel sunroof which could be specified as an optional extra.

Interior trim specification on the Type 3 was, as might be expected, designed for comfort. Lower door panels were covered in a textile material, while upper and quarter panels were finished in vinyl. Armrests on the doors were padded, as were the mouldings above the door and quarter panel trims. Thick sound-absorbent material was applied to the floor and covered with haircord carpet which extended as far as the front bulkhead, frame tunnel and sidemembers; seat belt anchorages were fitted as standard and the belt mounting plates were fixed under the quarter window and to the frame tunnel, near to the rear of the front seats. Headlining was of a leatherette material and swivelling sun visors were provided for both driver and passenger.

The dashboard of the Type 3 differed to that of the Type 1. Immediately ahead of the steering wheel three dials - fuel gauge on the left, speedometer in the centre and clock on the right - were accompanied by a mounting for a radio. Positioned alongside, and more or less in front of the passenger seat, was a circular speaker designed to match the style of the instrument dials. Push-buttons for the windscreen washers and the wipers were incorporated in the fascia, along with those for the parking lights and headlamps. A rheostat was also included, together with a variable speed controller for the windscreen wipers. (It must be mentioned that with 6-volt electrics wiper speed was often dependent on the state of battery charge). As for the windscreen washers, these were operated by compressed air and were connected to the valve on the spare wheel in the nose of the luggage compartment. This was something of a curious system, though already employed, to good effect, on Citroën's DS.

In the doors, side pockets added to the refinement, but it was the Type 3's luggage capacity that was most appealing. Apart from being able to drop the rear seat squab to form a capacious baggage rack, a parcel shelf behind the rear seat was also provided. Due to the design of both the engine and the engine compartment, it was possible to utilise a purpose-built compartment above the engine for luggage storage. (To gain access to the engine, the floor of the compartment hinged upwards to expose the mechanical running gear). All this was in addition to the front boot which offered a luggage capacity of 7 cubic feet. The Type 3's total luggage capacity amounted to 22 cubic feet (0.63m^3) but Volkswagen went further and assured potential customers it was possible to fill the spaces with 14 pieces of luggage, including a hat box! "Enough to tour Europe for weeks" was VW's final message.

The front compartment, as in the case of Type 1 cars, housed the fuel tank, the capacity of which was 8.8 gallons (41 litres), spare wheel and

The Type 3 Karmann Ghia boasted three luggage compartments. (Author's collection)

tools; in addition, both the windscreen washer bottle, connected to the spare wheel, and brake fluid reservoir were placed under the front bonnet.

At the heart of the Type 3 Karmann Ghia was the 1500 Volkswagen engine, the same as that which powered the VW Type 3 Saloon. With its 1493cc capacity the engine had a maximum output of 45bhp at 3800rpm, which propelled the Karmann Ghia up to 87mph (139.2km/h). Although an improvement on previous performance, this still did not put the car anywhere near the sports car league. It was not so much the maximum speed that was important as acceleration through the gears. *Road & Track* magazine put the car through its paces and achieved the quarter mile from a standing start in under 22 seconds, by which time the speedometer needle was hovering around 60mph (96km/h) with more power on hand. Fuel consumption, whilst important, was not crucial: 22-25mpg (13.5-11.5Lt/100km) was within the limits that purchasers of a delectable touring car might consider reasonable.

In concept, of course, the engine was entirely similar to all other Volkswagen 1500s. Tuning specialists - Okrasa, for one - immediately showed an interest in making the Karmann Ghia go faster, but many owners of both Type 1 and Type 3 cars must have wished that Volkswagen had given the car a little more performance in the first place. Interestingly, there is evidence that Ghia considered the possibility of producing its own bodies for a sports Volkswagen through O.S.I. at Turin, a company closely connected with Ghia which shared directors. In the event this did not happen.

The low profile of the 1500 engine demanded some mechanical modifications which included a re-designed cooling fan, moved from its position above the crankcase to the rear of the crankshaft. The fan itself was of smaller diameter although the amount of airflow had been increased. By re-designing the engine and modifying the layout, it had been possible to considerably reduce engine height, thereby providing extra luggage capacity. Incredibly, overall height of the engine was just 16 inches (407mm).

Volkswagen had designed the new 1493cc unit around the crankcase of the 1200 Beetle engine; the 4-bearing crankshaft was completely new, however. Specification included a Solex 32 PHN-1 carburettor and an all-synchromesh 4-speed gearbox.

On the exterior, Type 3 cars had anodised aluminium mouldings for the windscreen, rear window surrounds and quarter windows. Bumpers were chrome-plated, as were door handles, headlight rims, front quarterlight surrounds and the strips fitted below the doors.

The Type 3 Karmann Ghia was expensive for 1961: £1281 was equivalent to the price of *two* standard Beetles. It was more expensive than the Type 1 Coupé but something like £100 less than the Type 1 Convertible. The same amount of money could have purchased an MG 1600-engined TVR or a Renault Floride Hardtop. It would also have bought an Austin Healey

Here we see the Type 1's luggage capacity: the Type 3 Karmann Ghia just wins. (Author's collection)

3000 MkII with £100 to spare.

Three years after launch the Type 3 Karmann Ghia received its first major modification. Not only was the engine given a boost by altering the carburettor specification and compression ratio from 7.8:1 to 8.5:1, which produced 54bhp at 4200rpm, but the first right-hand drive models became available. Known as the 1500S engine, the Type 3's new power unit sounded as if it might have sporting inclinations but, alas it did not. Mechanical modifications were also made but these applied equally to the Type 3 Volkswagen Saloon; specific alterations to the heating and ventilation controls and steering wheel horn-push were implemented which were similarly applicable to Type 1 cars. A year later the semi-circular horn-push was re-introduced. Early cars can normally be identified by their wheels which, until the 1965 model year, had elongated slots between the hub and rim. Another identification feature is the shape of the badge on the nose panel: before 1965 this was square; later cars had the more familiar circular emblem.

Post-1966 modifications

Another power increase for Type 1 cars was welcomed by all, even though it was only a stop-gap before the 1500 engine from the Type 3 was fitted for 1967. The 1200 engine was showing its age but, by installing the Type 3 crankshaft into what was essentially the old crankcase, it was possible to boost capacity to 1285cc. The 'new' engine was dubbed the 1300 and, by

The Type 3 Karmann Ghia was something of a rarity in the UK. (Courtesy National Motor Museum)

A pristine Coupé seen in a car lot in California. Engine size eventually reached 1600, which helped pep-up the Karmann Ghia's performance. This particular car is a pre-1971 model. (Courtesy Martin McGarry)

raising the compression ratio to 7.3:1 from 7.0:1 and lengthening the stroke by 4mm (0.15 inches) to 69mm (2.75 inches), a more respectable 40bhp was achieved with the assistance of a new Solex carburettor. The maximum speed went up only marginally, by less than 3mph (4.8km/h) but, nevertheless, the new engine went some way towards silencing those critics who considered that the car should be capable of a more spirited performance and considerably higher speeds.

Some of the other changes to Type 1 cars might appear relatively minor but, in fact, were of some significance. Post-1966 model year cars can be identified by their wheels and wheel trims, as the pronounced hub caps of earlier vehicles had given way to a flatter design, and the wheels themselves were ventilated to allow more efficient cooling of the brakes. In the engine compartment, as well as the new 1300 motor, a revised air cleaner was responsible for repositioning of the battery to the opposite side of the engine. There were other mechanical modifications, too: the front suspension was given ball joints for the good reason that they were virtually maintenance-free.

As regards interior trim, the seats were re-designed for greater comfort and the steering wheel - though attractive in ivory-coloured plastic - was changed to black. The thumb-pushes for the horn, built into the steering wheel spokes, disappeared and were replaced by a semi-circular ring.

The 1966 model year was important to the Type 3 because, from August 1965, a new and uprated engine - from 1493cc to 1584cc - was specified. On paper, at least, there appeared, however, little change: the 1600 engine did not allow a higher maximum speed, but maximum power was reached a little earlier at 4000rpm instead of 4200rpm. The bore measurement was increased to 85.5mm (3.42 inches) from 83mm (3.32 inches) but, conversely, the compression ratio decreased from 8.5:1 to 7.7:1. While this may have benefited those motorists with access to less-refined petrol only, others were denied the higher performance they had been hoping for.

Every cloud has a silver lining, however, and although it could not go any faster than it had with the 1500S engine, the Karmann Ghia was now at least able to stop more quickly, thanks to increased braking power provided by disc brakes on the front wheels. Drum brakes were retained for the rear wheels and, at the same time, all four wheels were given vents to allow more efficient cooling of brake discs and drums. Matching alloy wheel trims were also available, and it was these which helped give the car its particularly smart appearance.

Criticism of the Type 1's poor power output, even with its uprated 1300 engine, continued. Lack of performance and a top speed that did not reach even 80mph (128km/h) were unimpressive, and a source of embarrassment was that its performance could be easily bettered by almost every other production car in existence, apart from those designed purely as economy machines. In order to improve the situation Volkswagen dispensed with the 1300 engine after only a year's service and, for 1967, replaced it with a slightly modified 1500 engine from the Type 3 Karmann Ghia. The 1500 engine was specified from August 1966; the only significant detail change from the version fitted to the Type 3 being the cooling fan, which was fitted on top of the engine.

To complement the new engine a number of mechanical and trim alterations were announced. Disc brakes continued to be specified for the front wheels while, overall, the braking system benefited from being uprated from a single to a dual circuit system. Modifications were also made to the rear suspension in order to provide better stability and reduce the effect of oversteer, a characteristic evident since the car had first been introduced. This comprised a spring device which ran across the car at the back of the cabin and connected the axle tubes to equalise the work of the torsion bars. A further improvement was widening of the rear track, whilst the wheels themselves were fitted to the hubs by four studs instead of five. Slightly less significant was the addition of a steering lock to aid vehicle security while, to give better visibility, new-type windscreen wipers were fitted. Inside the car, a woodgrain-type dashboard did not really enhance the cabin, although non-reflective black soft plastic switches were more safety-orientated. Adding the final touch to the trim, the Karmann Ghia script was incorporated on the fascia.

Type 3 cars for 1967 underwent

The end of the road for the Type 3 Karmann Ghia was reached in July 1969 after 42,498 examples had been built. This is an extremely nicely presented car. (Courtesy Martin McGarry)

a series of modifications, the most important being uprating of the electrics from 6 to 12-volts. Type 1 cars, however, had to wait a further year before receiving this luxury. By having a 12-volt electrical system it was possible to add a range of optional equipment to the car's specification, the most desirable being a heated rear window, a facility previously almost unthinkable. Improvements to trim were also made and, as a result, more comfortable seats were fitted which provided better ergonomics as well as being wider and more easily adjustable.

To assist driver comfort the gearchange was revised to provide both a shorter lever and more precise gate, the latter made possible by modification to the selector device. The door-locking mechanism was also changed, and inside the car push-knobs were fitted to the window sills of the doors. Cosmetically, the Type 3 received a woodgrain dashboard similar to Type 1 cars. Needless to say, this 'improvement' was not happily received.

As 12-volt electrics were made standard from August 1967 for the 1968 model year, Type 1 cars were furnished with a range of features and accessories not previously available. As well as easier starting, especially in winter, the complaints of glow-worm-like headlights ceased; 2-speed windscreen wipers were specified, as were hazard warning lamps, together with a cigar lighter. With regard to comfort, the front seats were re-designed to incorporate built-in head restraints.

By far the most adventurous innovation, however, was the introduction of the semi-automatic gearbox. The system worked extremely well but did not meet with universal acclaim. One of the reasons for this was that the driver still had to change gear manually although a clutch pedal was no longer necessary. A further reason was that it impaired performance and increased fuel consumption. Semi-automatic gearboxes were by no means unknown; a virtually identical system was available for the 1500 Beetle and could be specified for the 1300 a year later. Porsche used a similar gearbox on the 911 Sportomatic and a number of other cars offered varying equipment on a parallel theme.

Instead of the 4-speed manual gearbox, semi-automatic cars had a 3-speed gearchange coupled to a torque converter. The clutch was completely standard and, instead of being engaged manually, was controlled pneumatically via a switch connected to the gearlever. As soon as the gearshift was moved, a solenoid operated a vacuum control valve on the left-hand side of the engine which actuated the clutch. Whilst completely efficient, the semi-automatic system was not as popular as had been expected, which is why so few cars have survived with this option. The complaint was not so much about the transmission system itself but the disadvantages it had in the way of dragging down the car's speed and increasing its thirst.

There was one built-in advantage of the semi-automatic gearbox, however, as far as driveability of the Karmann Ghia was concerned. The system demanded double-jointed driveshafts, as found on the Porsche, and handling was considerably improved by the fact that these cars were fitted with additional semi-trailing arms which aided stability.

The 1500 engine powered Type 1 cars until August 1970 when, for the 1971 model year, the 1600 engine was fitted. During 1969 and until the 1971 models were announced, only relatively minor revisions to the model were made. These included a locking fuel filler flap, revised positioning of heater vents and modifications to the hood of the Convertible. The latter included specifying twin locking handles and glass in place of the plastic material for the rear window.

The Type 3 Karmann Ghia went a stage further with transmission specification than its Type 1 stablemate. Instead of employing a semi-automatic gearbox, a fully automatic system was made available as an option. As with the semi-automatic Type 1 cars, the automatic Type 3 enjoyed the revised rear suspension and double-jointed driveshafts. Safety was paramount and a collapsible steering column was fitted which complemented the soft-feel dashboard switches.

Performance-wise, 1968 was especially important as Bosch fuel injection became available as well as the 1600 engine with twin-port cylinder heads. Maximum speed reached a dizzy 90.1mph (145km/h), although the automatic gearbox brought the top speed down to 87mph (140km/h).

In the autumn of 1968 Volkswagen announced further changes for Type 3 cars for 1969. These were the final changes and, less than a year later in July 1969, production stopped. For 1969 the revised suspension previously utilised only on automatic cars was made standard for all Type 3s; hazard warning lights were fitted

Wrap-around indicators and bumpers were amongst the final modifications to the Karmann Ghia Type 1. (Courtesy Martin McGarry)

A pre-1971 Convertible poses alongside a post-1971 Coupé. Note the differing frontal treatment - apart, that is, from the American specification bumpers on the Convertible. (Courtesy Martin McGarry)

and coincided with the introduction of re-designed rear lamps. Trim embellishments were also revised and the last Type 3s can be identified by their flatter hub caps.

Type 1 cars continue

Before the 1600 engine was fitted to the Type 1 Coupé and Convertible, minor revisions included standardisation of radial-ply tyres. When the 1600 engine was fitted to the Type 1 Karmann Ghia it was equipped with twin-port cylinder heads from the outset. Other modifications included a new type of oil cooler, which assisted in making the engine more efficient, and performance benefited considerably. Maximum speed was the main improvement and increased to 84mph (135km/h). The 1600 engine was devised from the 1500 unit but with cylinders bored out to 85.5mm; the 1500's crankshaft was utilised and produced a compression ration of 7.5:1. Semi-automatic cars were slower, reaching only 78mph (125km/h) and fuel consumption suffered into the bargain.

Large section bumpers and wrap-around indicators are features of post-1971 cars. (Courtesy Martin McGarry)

In its 1600 guise - identified by the 1600 badge on the engine compartment lid - the Type 1 Coupé and Convertible was never more sophisticated, especially with its ultimate trim level which included a new padded steering wheel, with 4 spokes instead of the more familiar 2. For 1972 the fascia was updated, the matt black finish eliminating any risk of reflection in the windscreen. Safety measures did not end there: new rear lights were fitted and replaced those introduced only the previous year when reversing lamps had been incorporated. New front indicators of an elongated wrap-around design were introduced in 1971.

In the interests of safety and passenger protection, 1972 model year cars were fitted with a new type of bumper. Known as the 'Europa' bumper, these were larger in section and incorporated a rubber cushioning pad designed to absorb minor impacts. Intended for only relatively slight shocks, such as parking incidents, the bumpers could, nevertheless withstand a 25mph (40km/h) impact.

Late cars were fitted with improved exhaust systems and wider section tyres; nickel-plated silencers made for more robust exhausts and 600x15 tubeless radials placed more rubber on the road surface.

Having started its production career in 1955, the Karmann Ghia had, by the early 1970s, become a little outmoded; certainly the styling was as chic and elegant as ever but the original concept was losing strength and rear-engined cars were nearing

The Karmann Ghia was also produced in Brazil, although this car was pictured in California. Note the fastback styling unique to Brazilian-produced cars. (Courtesy Martin McGarry)

their sell-by date. Renault had already turned its back on rear-drive models, fearing their appeal was waning, and Volkswagen had sought a new direction with the newly-announced front-wheel drive K70.

Both Karmann and Volkswagen knew that the days of the Karmann Ghia were numbered and sought a suitable replacement. The Beetle, too, was nearing the limit of its useful life although, even now, and few would have guessed that, in 1998, a New Beetle would be introduced to huge acclaim.

Production of the Karmann Ghia ended in June 1974 when the last cars destined for the American market rolled off the assembly line on the 21st of that month. European market production had already come to a halt at the end of 1973 when the last cars left Osnabrück on December 21st.

In retrospect

As soon as the last Karmann Ghia left the assembly hall at Osnabrück its replacements - the Scirocco and the Golf Cabrio - were already waiting to be built. Successful cars in their own right, the Scirocco and Golf, nevertheless, did not possess the same charisma as the Karmann Ghia; the unique curvaceousness of the Type 1 body design made it a breed apart. The Type 3 Karmann Ghia, too, displayed a particular elegance and deserved to have sold in greater numbers than it did.

Sales of the Type 1 Coupé peaked in 1965 when as many as 28,387 cars were produced; the Convertible, which was built in much smaller numbers, had its best sales in 1971 with 6565 vehicles leaving Osnabrück. The majority of Convertibles were sent to America where open-top motoring was appreciated far more than in Europe. As for the Type 3, this sold in only half the number of the Type 1 Convertible, making the car something of a rarity. Its best year was 1964 when 7367 cars were produced; after that sales progressively declined.

The Brazilian connection

Not quite all Karmann Ghia production had ended by 1974 and it was left to South America to continue flying the Karmann flag, although the Brazilian product was not too much like its Osnabrück counterpart.

Volkswagen in Brazil was established in 1953 but it was not until four years later, in 1957, that the first completely Brazilian-built Volkswagens emerged from the factory at Sao Bernado do Campo. Between 1953 and 1957 Volkswagens were assembled at the plant from parts supplied in kit form from Wolfsburg and other factories. Production was not extensive and, between these dates, less than 3000 cars were produced.

Convertibles are much sought-after by enthusiasts in the UK. This late model is particularly well-presented. (Courtesy Martin McGarry)

Compared to the Type 1 Coupé and Convertible, of which 444,300 examples were built, the Type 3 Coupé was produced in such few numbers that it was always assured exclusivity. Between 1961 and 1969, only 42,498 Type 3s were manufactured. Built as a Coupé only, a Convertible version of the Type 3 had originally been planned and was featured in the original sales material. Problems regarding lack of torsional stiffness in the bodyshell resulted in abandonment of a Convertible variant. (Courtesy Volkswagen)

Within ten years of the plant turning out locally manufactured vehicles, the production rate was running at 95,000 cars a year.

As output increased, Karmann opened a factory near the Volkswagen plant in 1960 which was known as Karmann Ghia do Brazil S.A. Production of locally-built Type 1 Coupés, designated SP1, commenced in 1962 but it was not until six years later that the Convertible, the SP2, went into production. Both cars, which resembled the Osnabrück product, were built until 1971 when Karmann announced a quite spectacular fastback Coupé based upon the Type 3 chassis. Production of SP1 and SP2 cars amounted to an impressive 28,323 vehicles.

The Brazilian built 2+2 Fastback was quite unlike anything built at Osnabrück; the front wings were reminiscent of the Type 3 Saloon and Fastback, whilst rear wings had more of an affinity with those on Type 1 cars. Apart from the running gear, this is where any similarity with either the Type 1 or Type 3 cars ended. Elongated 'nostrils' adorned the front panel and appeared more like radiator air intakes than fresh air vents; the front indicator lamps resembled those found on the last built Type 1 Karmann Ghias.

Large wrap-around rear lights were a particular feature of the car and the engine air intake louvres were positioned very neatly at the rear edge of the Fastback panel, below the lift-up engine compartment lid.

The TC, as the Fastback was known, was built in relatively large numbers, although it did not quite match the production rate of the SP1 and SP2. Even so, at 23,577 units, production was more than half of that of the Type 3 Karmann Ghia produced at Osnabrück.

Karmann Ghia in America

By far the largest single export market for the Karmann Ghia was North America. Effectively, the only car exported to the United States was the Type 1, as the Type 3 was never officially available there. Something in excess of 40 per cent of the Karmann Ghia's total output was destined for the USA, where the cars were treated with reverence.

In total, 538,698 Karmann Ghias were built, including the cars produced in Brazil; the exact number of cars despatched to America is debatable, especially as one source of research claims as many as 288,651 vehicles - 59 per cent of Osnabrück's output - was shipped across the Atlantic. For such a large market Volkswagen and Karmann had to take into account local legislation and therefore some specification appeared different to that of the European market cars.

The most obvious difference between American and European cars concerns the bumpers, as the American version had tall overriders and a separate protection rail above the main bumper bar. A number of other differences are also evident; sealed beam headlamp units were specified from the beginning of export deliveries and tail lights were fitted with red lenses only and did not have amber segments as did European cars. Front indicator lamps were also different and were equipped with white lenses only.

To assist in identification of model years, a chronology is included in the appendices.

KARMANN Ghia

3
LIVING WITH A KARMANN GHIA

What is it that makes the Karmann Ghia a legend of recent motoring history? In a world where there are many beautiful motor cars, why is the Karmann Ghia singled out as special?

Perhaps it's the car's rare qualities of exquisite design coupled with hand-crafted coachwork? Possibly it is the Porsche-developed chassis which could easily have been the basis of a sports car? With a pedigree that all can admire, the Karmann Ghia's strength is not so much an aggressive turn of speed as competent performance and robust reliability.

It is important to remember that the Karmann Ghia was never intended as an out-and-out sports car; neither was it meant to compete alongside such cars as the Porsche and the like. No, its objective was to be an appealing and attractive alternative to the Beetle which, for hundreds of thousands of families, had provided truly admirable motoring. Characteristically, the Karmann Ghia may look and feel more of a sports car than a completely functional family saloon; in truth, of course, it drives like a normal Volkswagen.

Karmann Ghia owners are a

Although the Karmann Ghia may have the look and feel of a sportscar, it was nevertheless intended as a stylish alternative to the Volkswagen Beetle. (Courtesy Martin McGarry)

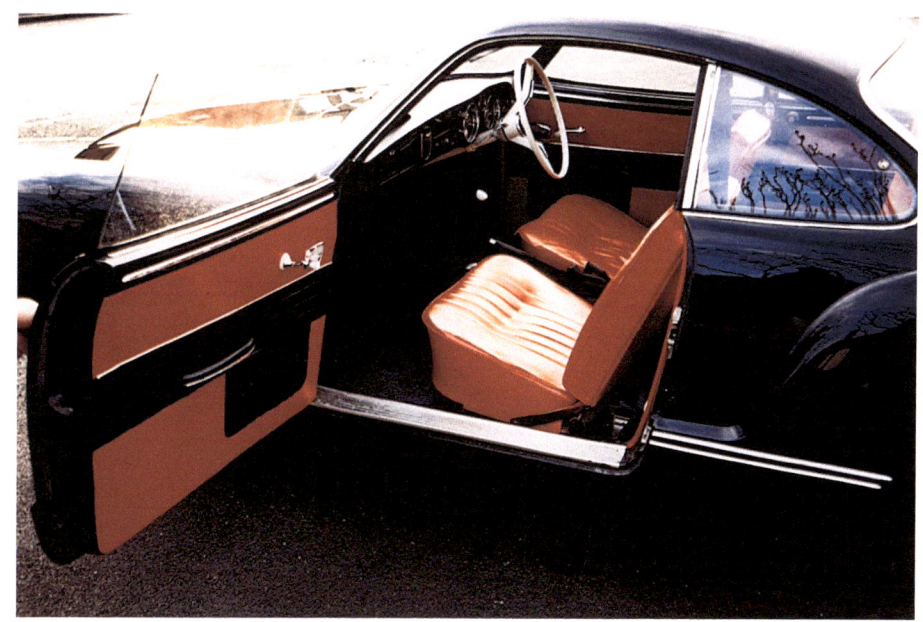

Inside a Karmann Ghia the low-slung seats are inviting and comfortable. (Courtesy Martin McGarry)

fortunate breed. Just one look at the classified advertisements in any classic car magazine is enough to show the large following that Volkswagen enjoys; a browse through a VW enthusiast periodical will reveal the plethora of specialists and concerns dedicated to maintaining the marque.

The Karmann Ghia is alive and well, its survival in numbers due not only to the loyal enthusiasts who brave all the rigours of keeping their cars in good order, but also to the fact that so many cars were exported to America, and California in particular. Had the Karmann Ghia been restricted to its native Germany and mainland Europe, it's unlikely to have survived in the numbers it has.

Driving a Karmann Ghia

Open the doors of a Karmann Ghia and it will be instantly noticeable just how low-slung and inviting the seats appear, in keeping with the car's gracefulness. Ideal for long periods behind the wheel, the seats are firm and supportive, and wide enough not to feel restrictive in any way with much fore and aft adjustment for complete comfort. If there is any criticism of the seating it is that it could be too low-slung which, whilst fine for tall drivers, is not so good for shorter people who sometimes are forced to 'peer' over the rather high-mounted steering wheel.

Because of the Karmann Ghia's close relationship to the Beetle, expect it to drive like one - but only up to a point. The Karmann's extra weight is noticeable, compensated for, to a degree, by the car's aerodynamic shape. Expect the Convertible version to be different again due to its even greater weight disadvantage, which would normally suggest slightly reduced performance. In fact, the Convertible is a fraction quicker, both in acceleration and top speed. Approximately 2mph (3.2km/h) faster than the Coupé, the Convertible reaches maximum speed a couple of seconds quicker.

It is a matter of opinion whether the Coupé or Convertible Type 1 is the more attractive. Both Type 1 cars drive in a similar fashion but there are certain differences. The Coupé has a tauter feel, while the Convertible has a tendency to flex a little over rough surfaces, not unexpected considering the loss of torsional stiffness normally afforded by the steel roof.

The cars' pedigree is immediately obvious upon getting behind the wheel;

The Karmann Ghia is often dubbed the 'poor man's Porsche', something that neither Karmann Ghia or Porsche enthusiasts would agree with. Note the non-standard wheel trims. (Courtesy Martin McGarry)

The Type 3 Karmann Ghia. Although a very desirable car, the model never had the same appeal as the Type 1. (Courtesy National Motor Museum)

there is no mistaking the quality and finish only found in a hand-crafted motor car. Early cars have much more of a spartan feel compared to the late Karmann Ghias but this is not detrimental. Late Karmann Ghias enjoy numerous extras, the result of almost twenty years of continuous development and technology. In the majority of cases anyone purchasing a Karmann Ghia for the first time will buy a late model, if only because availability dictates this. Early cars tend to have their loyal devotees.

What makes driving a Karmann such a pleasurable experience? Firstly, it is knowing that the car is going to start, normally first time, every time; gone is the worry of water-cooling with its risk of overheating in the summer and freezing in the winter. Secondly, the proven drivetrain makes for surefootedness and agility. Certainly there is a tendency towards oversteer and knowing how to compensate for this is all part of the pleasure of driving a Volkswagen. The steering itself, although perhaps not as direct as rack and pinion, is nevertheless perfectly responsive and delightfully light. Forget about the gearshift, the gearbox is superbly well-mannered and allows quick and easy changes.

On starting the engine the familiar VW flat-four makes itself heard, especially when cold, but as the engine gets warmer so the noise level reduces considerably. The noise is not so much to do with the Volkswagen engine in particular but air-cooled engines in general. As the Karmann Ghia developed over the years, so the cabin insulation became all the more effective, which helped dampen excess noise. Hence, a late car will be that much quieter than an early example.

So far the emphasis in this chapter has been on the Type 1 cars, but what about the Type 3 which was always in Coupé form, apart, that is, from one-off conversions? Comparing the two the Type 1 is definitely the more sporting-looking and its cabin certainly reflects the charms of the European 50s/60s GT sports car.

The Type 3 feels far less like a performance car, due, in part, to interior styling with a vast glass area. The airy cabin and broad plush seats are far removed from the Type 1's cosy atmosphere. Gone, to a certain extent, are the original aerodynamics; to be somewhat cruel to what was, after all, an excellent body design, it suffered from a touch of austerity. Nevertheless, the Type 3 remains something of an enigma to the majority of VW/Karmann enthusiasts and this, no doubt, stems from its limited production and resultant rarity. Whilst many Volkswagen enthusiasts regard Type 1 cars with affection, glorying in its sculptured beauty, there is a tendency to dismiss Type 3 cars, which is sad considering the model's pedigree.

The Type 3's road manners are quite different to those of the Type 1. This may seem surprising, especially to the uninitiated who might expect the handling to be similar, bearing in mind the close relationship between the two cars. Less agile than the Type 1, the Type 3 is more sedate, but that does not mean it is boring - just the opposite, in fact.

Type 1 cars can be driven through bends at high speed, but the Type 3 has to be treated with greater respect. Sure, it's possible to get the Type 3 through tortuous bends, but it needs a different technique; power has to be applied once the car has been thrown into the bend and in order to leave the bend at high speed. Early Type 3s were made more cumbersome by cross-ply tyres; once radials were specified handling was surer.

In a manner, driving a Type 3, with its relaxed bearing, could almost be classed as therapeutic. The high top gearing ensured that the Type 3 was a true motorway - or autobahn - cruiser and the transmission's long-leggedness allowed flat-out motoring over considerable distances. Although taking fast long distance cruising in its stride, getting through the gears was more of a fuss. By the time a true sports car had reached 60mph (96km/h) or more, the Type 3 was just about staggering towards 40mph (64km/h).

For all its class the Type 3 dashboard was nevertheless quite basic, so do not expect a plethora of dials. A criticism always has been that the car did not sport a tachometer, and certainly this would have been much more useful than the ornate clock it does have. As for visibility, this was a lot better than in most other cars of the period. The slim pillars and huge windows allowed superb all-round vision and was a huge improvement over the Ford Capri, with which it was compared by *Car* magazine.

As with all Karmann Ghias the Type 3 suffers from problems with ventilation. This can be exacerbated in hot weather with the sun glaring into

This Coupé may appear to be a viable restoration project, but closer examination revealed the condition of the car to be such that any restoration would have been a major undertaking - if possible at all. (Courtesy Martin McGarry)

Early Type 1 Coupés are rare and desirable cars, and the example pictured here is in excellent condition. This particular vehicle is one of the oldest surviving, and dates from early 1956. (Courtesy Martin McGarry).

the car through the huge windscreen that extends almost into the roof. However, there are a host of fine features which make the car wholly endearing, not least of which is ample luggage capacity. If the Type 1 had limited baggage space, the Type 3 had plenty and boasted two 'boots'. In addition, of course, the platform behind the front seats provided even more luggage space.

Buying a Karmann Ghia
What should an enthusiast be aware of when considering the purchase of a Karmann Ghia? What are the tell-tale signs that a car is not all it's purported to be? What are the car's weaknesses and what should be paid? Whether or not a private sale is better than seeking the advice of a Karmann or Volkswagen specialist is another question. The answers to these and other questions follow.

Due to the sheer number of cars produced by Karmann, it is most likely that a Type 1 Karmann Ghia - and a Coupé at that - will be chosen. It is not that this particular car is considered any better than either the Convertible or Type 3, just that there were almost three times as many of this model as all the others combined.

As a classic car the Karmann Ghia is a popular choice; not only are its contours beguiling, but original quality can mean a prolonged life and makes the car a promising restoration project.

Falling in love with a classic car is easy enough. The stark reality of not being able to source a particular spare part, or find a specialist willing to undertake the necessary work, often means that the honeymoon is short. As far as the Karmann Ghia is concerned, mechanical parts -

The Karmann Ghia may not be a practical car when it comes to transporting a family with the usual plethora of luggage. There is, nevertheless, a solution; depending, of course, on finding a suitable donor car. (Courtesy Martin McGarry)

certainly for the later cars - are still relatively plentiful and a number of body panels can usually be acquired, thanks to a network of specialists supplying remanufactured parts.

Buying a Karmann Ghia through a private sale means the potential purchaser will have to know exactly what to look for. A car that looks good on the surface may be a viable DIY restoration project but purchasing through a reputable and recognised specialist will usually avoid this worry. Expect, however, to pay a slightly higher price. If you are in Europe, one alternative is to acquire a car from America, particularly California, the hunting ground for many a good Karmann because of the number of cars originally exported there and the dry climate it enjoys. The last option is not one to be considered lightly unless dealing through an experienced agent able to provide a comprehensive service. It is possible to travel to America to find a car; it can be rewarding and a holiday into the bargain, but it could also spell disaster.

Possibly one of the car's keenest enthusiasts is Martin McGarry. Apart from editing *Karmann Komment*, the Karmann Ghia Owners' Club magazine, Martin very successfully runs his own business which specialises in importing and restoring Karmann Ghias. A visit to Martin McGarry's Motorworks in Mansfield, Nottinghamshire, soon revealed the commitment of at least one specialist concerned in the preservation of the marque. It's not only the Karmann Ghia that Martin specialises in, he also deals with the Karmann Beetle Cabriolet and has a high regard for the Type 3 Volkswagen, an example of which he currently owns.

In conversation with Martin, the question of how much should be paid for a Karmann Ghia arose very quickly. It is possible to find very poor examples advertised for around £1000, but these will be no more than wrecks from which a few parts might be utilised. As a rule of thumb, do not expect much for your money for under £3500, which will probably buy not much more than a shell requiring major restoration. Most of the trim will be missing, including bumpers, and remember that side trims alone cost a minimum of £400. And it goes without saying that the car will not have a genuine MoT roadworthiness certificate if applicable.

Imported to Europe from California, a batch of Karmann Ghias en-route for restoration. (Courtesy Martin McGarry)

Below: Some cars may be so extensively corroded that it is uneconomical to repair or restore them. (Courtesy Martin McGarry)

Up to £4000-£4500 should purchase a car that actually runs. It will probably be left-hand drive, will not have a current MoT certificate if appropriate and will almost certainly require a substantial amount of welding. For a reasonable car which may require only minor work, including the fitting of some missing items of trim, it will be necessary to pay £5000-£7000.

A nicely presented imported car will almost certainly cost at least £7000-£7500, but if it is a right-hand drive model in a similar condition, consider spending something in excess of up to £8000. In the region of £10,000 will undoubtedly purchase a desirable example but, if it's a convertible you're after, expect to pay a premium of at least £2500-£3000 in each of the categories. When buying a car, look for one that is as rust-free as possible, as complete as can be expected and with the most original trim. Looking at advertisements, it is evident that typical prices range from £15,000 to £24,000 for cars in good condition, and sometimes much higher for early, thus rare, RHD examples that have been restored to concours condition. Beware that some cars, despite reflecting a high quality restoration, might be over valued by their proud owners.

Martin McGarry's main business is importing Karmann Ghias and Karmann Cabriolets to the UK, mainly from California, and restoring them. Once delivered to the United Kingdom the cars are subjected to a rigorous check in Martin's workshops, where all repair and restoration is undertaken before sale.

Right-hand drive cars in Britain suffer from rust; historically, some Karmanns have undergone poor quality repairs just to keep them on the road. Parts have always been costly, and even 35 years ago a replacement wing would have cost as much as £400. Volkswagen agents were, at that time, the only suppliers of Karmann parts, which made availability a little more difficult. Relatively slow sales in the United Kingdom meant that there are few early, cigar-shaped Karmann Ghias available, those with the small nostrils and more prominent front wings.

If a Karmann Ghia has suffered extensive rot it may well be that the car is uneconomical to restore. That said, miracles have been achieved against the odds. Rot can be exacerbated if the car has been previously damage-repaired; if repairs to the bodywork have not been properly leaded it is likely water will have penetrated the repair, causing extensive rusting. Front and rear shunts are the most common cause of accident damage. The Karmann Ghia's pronounced nose tends to cave-in under impact; at the rear there is a much greater risk of more serious damage which can lead to creasing of the whole area around the

Front and rear shunts can cause extensive damage. Front sections are hollow and cave-in easily ... (Courtesy Martin McGarry)

... whilst rear shunts can crease the entire engine compartment. (Courtesy Martin McGarry

engine and gearbox. A good indication of whether a car has been accident repaired is the condition of the chrome trim strip along the bodywork - it should be straight!

So, who buys a Karmann Ghia today? Martin McGarry's customers are mostly of the younger generation, keen to re-kindle the era of the fifties, sixties and seventies. The Karmann is something of an enigma; a hand-built car based upon a mass-manufactured product, which itself has cult status. Martin McGarry offers his customers a personal service: not only does he oversee all mechanical work and bodywork himself, he also travels to the United States in search of the right vehicles to import. Normally in a year Martin will arrange up to five or six consignments of cars; with six cars to a container he can reckon on taking up to 40 cars, including a few which he sources in Europe. In Martin's opinion the best cars originate from Texas or Arizona.

Even with the kind climate it does not mean that dry state American Karmann Ghias are without problems - they suffer in different ways to their European counterparts. The heat can play havoc with interior trim and the Convertible's hood is particularly vulnerable as the vinyl material tends to crack beyond repair, requiring complete replacement. It's possible to find cars whose hoods have never been raised but, even so, it's a good bet they will require renewing. Even if the bodywork is in fair order it is likely that some mechanical restoration will be needed, and sometimes extensive repair.

If hoods are at risk so, too, are carpets and seats, the heat destroying them completely sometimes. Fortunately, most of the materials are available, if sometimes at high cost. When selling or restoring a car he has imported, Martin often spends huge amounts of time locating the trim components; even getting trim back to original shape and condition can take many hours of tedious effort.

For Martin, selling the cars is not a problem but it does matter what colour the vehicle is. Orange, in the sixties once a popular shade for everything from cars to kitchens, now has limited attraction.

When a car first arrives from the States Martin knows that a number of jobs will be compulsory because of its lifestyle and location. Lights will require changing and these alone cost £450-£500 a pair; all mechanical rubbers will have to be changed, as will brake hoses, brake shoes and pads. Windscreen wipers and wiper arms always need renewing and items of trim almost certainly need replacement. The heater mechanism - possibly never used - will be useless and, without exception, the tyres will have to be replaced with new ones.

The pitfalls - and what to expect from the body beautiful

Whilst *virtually* everything is available for the Karmann Ghia, certain parts - especially body panels like doors and trim components - can be difficult to source. Often components have to be imported and may be expensive as a result.

Do not take the view that because the Karmann Ghia is hand-built it will last forever. However good initial build quality is, it is a fact of motor industry history that rustproofing was not as advanced when the Karmann was made as it is now. Earlier cars have the disadvantage of less powerful engines and the perils of 6-volt electrics. For the rigours of today's motoring it has to be said that 6-volts are hardly up to the job and can cause all sorts of difficulties. Starting - especially when the car has stood idle for long periods - can be tortuous and the amount of light emitted from the headlamps is not much better than a glimmer only a glow-worm would be proud of. A breakthrough at least is the supply of 6-volt halogen headlamps.

Most components for the Karmann Ghia are still obtainable from one source or another - which is just as well! (Courtesy Martin McGarry)

A guide to what to look for when considering a Karmann Ghia would be similar for both Coupés and Convertibles. In the case of the latter, there are specific points to watch for. Convertibles have a nasty habit of rusting from the inside and, once damage is visible, it is already too late to effect repair other than by major surgery. Water tends to drip from the hood and collect in the door bottoms, unable to escape due to blocked drain holes. If a door is rotten beyond repair, a secondhand item will have to be sourced as new door panels are unavailable.

Watch for tears in the hood also: apart from obvious damage, water dripping onto the floor over a length of time can cause havoc. The stress of the hood presents problems, too, especially with very high mileage cars; the metalwork taking most of the flexing can, under extreme circumstances, split apart.

Damage to the hood of a Convertible is likely to be expensive to repair, but check the condition of the frame as well

Convertibles are nice to look at but it's essential to thoroughly check their condition, especially sills and strengthening panels. (Courtesy Martin McGarry)

If major surgery is necessary on a Convertible it can be a long and laborious job. (Courtesy Martin McGarry)

Some Karmann Ghias require more work than others ... (Courtesy Martin McGarry)

as the material. Convertibles rely upon strengthening panels built into the sills to compensate for loss of torsional stiffness provided by the steel roof of Coupés; if the sills have rotted, it is going to be a long and laborious job to make the car good. A tell-tale sign of impending trouble is signalled by the gap between the doors and rear quarter panels: it should be even, but beware the car with a gap that is narrower at the top than the bottom.

Starting from the ground up it is important to check the floorpan and sills. The floorpan, although modified, is very similar to that of the Beetle and,

... and sills and floorpan are especially vulnerable. (Courtesy Martin McGarry)

as a result, means that the Karmann Ghia suffers the same problems. Much of these are caused by water trapped on the floorpan's ribbed platform. Apart from the risk of rusted bolts (which can impede removal of the body from the chassis) there is also the danger of footwells with little or no metal between the road surface and the interior carpet. Should the floorpan appear very rotted, do not try and lift the car by the usual side jack: apart from a risk to safety, even more damage may be caused by trying this.

The Karmann Ghia has its wings welded onto the main structure, unlike the Karmann Beetle Cabriolet, the wings of which are bolted in place. This Convertible is the subject of a nut-and-bolt restoration. (Courtesy Martin McGarry)

The sills can present their own problems. As well as being vulnerable they are also very difficult to source if replacement is necessary and, therefore, will be an expensive item. Acting as a partial support for the car they must be expertly welded into place and are all the more complicated as they carry the integral heater ducts from the engine to the cabin.

A sure indication of impending rot in the sills and floorpan will be the condition of the front and rear wings. A continuous build-up of dampness caused by the collection of wet road debris will sooner, rather than later, lead to rotting around the wheelarches. Extreme problems can be experienced with the front inner wings which have a tendency to rot outwards, and this is most apparent where the inner wing meets adjacent panels. Any work carried out in this region is likely to be awkward and very time-consuming.

Rear wings suffer similar problems to those at the front though, fortunately, fabricated repair section panels are available from Karmann Ghia specialists. Nevertheless, look for serious rotting behind the base of the C-post. Ahead of the rear wings, and just in front of the wheelarch, there can normally be found a round-shaped metal plug. The purpose of this is to provide access to the rear torsion bars, but be careful if this hole has been plated over as it will indicate a less than desirable repair.

Pay attention also to the rear valance which has a habit of attracting mud and moisture to its side and upper edges; if not regularly cleared of trapped dirt it will have an adverse affect on the wings as well as the engine platform.

It is essential to investigate the rear inner wings which are prone to decay. Take a good look at the battery and the panel beneath it; the result of leaking acid will be all too evident. Check at the same time the platform beneath the rear seat as it has been known for it to completely rot away.

Unlike the Beetle, which has bolt-on wing panels, the Karmann Ghia has its wings welded onto the main body structure. If work is necessary in these areas allow for the extra expense and time required to effect a repair.

Whilst at the rear of the car take a look at the engine compartment cover which may have rust bubbles along the lower edge. Although it may be possible

59

The Karmann Ghia Owners' Club (GB) guide to checking over your Karmann Ghia. (Courtesy Karmann Ghia Owners' Club)

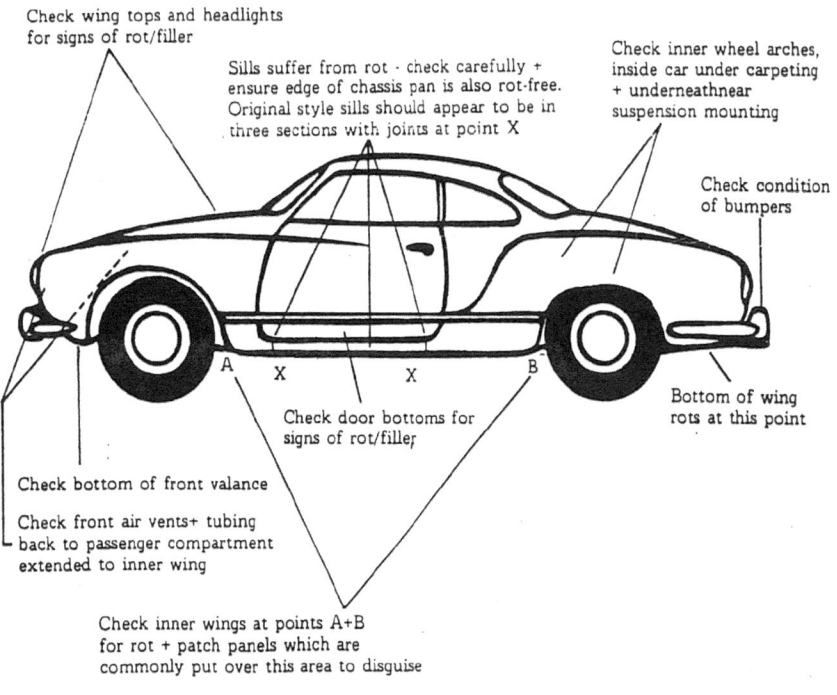

 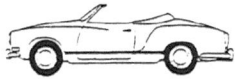 

to carry out a perfectly efficient repair, it must always be considered whether the rot has travelled too far, making replacement the only viable option. Luckily, new panels can be sourced but will probably have to be imported.

The condition of the Karmann Ghia's doors is of paramount importance. New doors are not now available so it is essential that existing door panels are repairable. The task of searching through autojumbles galore, or the possibility of having to acquire a donor vehicle, is daunting. Blocked drain holes, as already discussed, are the main cause of damage as rot spreads to the outside, so it's important they are kept in good condition. In addition, doors are vulnerable to accident damage.

As with the engine compartment cover, the luggage bonnet is at risk from the dreaded rust bug. Here, the area most prone to rot is the leading edge, but take a good look at the whole structure. The double-skinned frame can fall prey to corrosion which, at worst, will be unrepairable, making it necessary to fit a new panel which will probably have to be imported. With the bonnet lid open it's a good idea to inspect the nose of the luggage compartment, especially the spare wheel tray. Rot is frequently found here and, if evident, the tray will need refabricating rather than repair as a matter of urgency.

The front end of the car can have suffered all sorts of damage and, as a result, can look a sorry sight. At worst a car can suffer the ignominy of missing one, and possibly both, of its headlamps, as well the nostril grilles; rust can extend from the front wheelarches to the headlamp posts and round to the nose cone itself. The joints between the front wings can be corroded to a great extent and the ingress of moisture and debris will have caused much damage. Obviously, such repair work is only for the dedicated enthusiast. A new nose cone will be an expensive outlay.

Type 3 Karmann Ghias, of which relatively few exist, generally suffer from the same problems as Type 1 cars. Rust is the main villain but what makes matters worse is the fact that little exists in the way of body panels and trim items. What does become available from time to time is therefore likely to be highly expensive, especially if in reasonable or good condition. Even more cost will be involved if the

Check that doors are not badly damaged: new doors are currently unavailable. (Courtesy Martin McGarry)

parts need restoration before they can be used.

The Type 3 was never officially exported to America although a small number were despatched across the Atlantic for publicity purposes. Type 3s in America have been especially imported from Europe by devotees of

The front of the car is susceptible to all sorts of damage. Rot is evident on the exterior, but the inside of the front panel could well be extensively damaged, too. (Courtesy Martin McGarry)

61

Bodywork repairs are likely to be expensive and time-consuming. (Courtesy Martin McGarry)

the marque. Finding a good example, even in California, is going to be difficult. To put locating a good Type 3 in its proper perspective, remember that out of the original 42,498 cars

The help of trim specialists may be necessary for damage such as this. (Courtesy Martin McGarry)

This dashboard may look good now ... (Courtesy Martin McGarry)

... but this is how it once was! (Courtesy Martin McGarry)

produced it is thought that only as few as 2500 and 3000 have survived worldwide.

Built only in Coupé form, Type 3s do not exist as Convertibles, apart from the prototype car in the Karmann museum. Any Type 3 Convertibles offered for sale will not be genuine and should be regarded with extreme caution.

The extent of rusting on both Types

If well looked after a Volkswagen engine can achieve 150,000 miles (240,000km). (Author's collection)

1 and 3 cars will normally be uniform; if a car has a badly corroded nose cone it stands to reason that other vulnerable areas will be similarly affected. As a point of interest do not take the roof as an indication of the car's condition - roofs are generally rust-free.

When looking at a car, inspect the interior; if seats need re-trimming or carpets replacing, remember to allow for this in the final price. Carpets may be difficult to obtain, they are available for left-hand drive cars only and will therefore have to be specially made or modified if you have a rhd model. Window winders, door handles and locks may seem a minor point at the time of contemplating the purchase of a car, but if they are missing or not working it can be a headache later. Interior trim parts may also be hard to come by and often it is the obscure item that is the most difficult to locate. Instruments and switches should be complete and working correctly; it is fortunate they are of similar design to those fitted to the Beetle.

Finally, on the question of bodywork, remember that, due to the Karmann Ghia's intricate pattern of small body panels - Karmann did not possess large presses - each part is dependent upon the strength of its welds. Any work carried out on the car's bodywork structure may require the use of special jigs, and will possibly need the attention of a specialist with a good knowledge of the car's construction.

Before going to view a car, try and take a look at a perfect car; gaps between panels and doors, the quality-sounding thud as a door closes, all are virtues of a fine motor car. If the car being viewed has American specification bumpers do not immediately conclude that the vehicle has been imported from the USA. Double bumpers, as found on American export cars, are a popular accessory with enthusiasts and a number of owners have fitted them in preference to the original type fitted to European cars.

Whilst most parts for the Karmann

Access to the Karmann Ghia's engine compartment is easy enough. This picture shows a car in the process of restoration with the engine removed. (Courtesy Martin McGarry)

Ghia are generally available, it is wise to appreciate that these items often have to be imported from Germany or America. It will be a sensible precaution to join either the Karmann Ghia Owners Club or one of the other Volkswagen clubs which will have the facilities to give further advice on spares availability and specialist services.

Running gear

The mechanical design of the Karmann Ghia, as with the Beetle, is amongst the most rugged and durable of any motor car. The sheer number of Volkswagens produced has ensured an abundance of available spares and, even in the mid-1990s, the Beetle was still produced in Mexico.

Lifting the engine compartment lid will immediately give an idea of the condition of the running gear. A grimy, uncared-for engine bay will suggest that very little - perhaps only essential - maintenance work has been carried out. If this is the case but the bodywork and, hopefully, interior trim, is relatively sound and as rust-free as can be expected, do not immediately dismiss the vehicle on the condition of its running gear alone. Ready availability of mechanical spares and component parts will make for a relatively straightforward restoration project.

A point in the Karmann Ghia's favour is the excellent access to the engine compartment and reasonable space in which to work. The flat-four, air-cooled engine is familiar enough but do not expect it to last forever, regardless of claims that it is unburstable. It does have its weaknesses even though a well-maintained unit can cope with in excess of 150,000 miles without major attention.

If trouble does exist with the boxer engine it is as likely to be in the form of the dreaded 'dropped valve' on the 3rd cylinder; the problem can usually be traced to the exhaust valve and is more often than not a result of under-cooling. That the 3rd cylinder receives the least amount of cool air is a well-known shortcoming which can be exacerbated by excessively long periods of flat-out driving. A valve head can drop into the cylinder because the valves are constructed from two parts welded together, and the joint can be affected by overheating. In the most extreme cases complete engine failure can be the result of a dropped valve.

A leakage of oil around the pushrod tubes need not be too serious, although will normally indicate that the car has a high mileage. You will hear erroneous stories of Beetle engines being good for only 100,000 miles, however, contemplate an engine re-build only when absolutely necessary. If the oil leakage from the pushrod tubes is modest, it would be a false economy to consider stripping the engine. If the amount of spillage is high the only solution is to replace the rubber pushrod seals. If necessary, specialist advice can be sought in this respect.

Listen for any unusual noises from the engine, but remember that, when starting from cold, the unit will tend to clatter until it has settled down. Any unaccountable rumble may simply be a leaking exhaust but the cause could be far worse, such as worn bearings. With the engine switched off, grasp the crankshaft pulley wheel with both hands and, if there is any discernible movement, the signs are that an engine overhaul will be necessary due to worn bearings.

Cracked cylinder heads can make for very sluggish performance, accompanied by a distinctive noise not unlike that of a steam locomotive with leaky valve gear. Later twin-port engines are especially prone to damage of this sort and, if there is any doubt whatsoever about the cylinder heads, it is best to seek specialist advice.

By its nature the engine will puff out some blue smoke on initial starting. Volkswagen engines tend to run smoothly after only a few moments but, should smoking persist, especially on acceleration, it is usually a sign of piston ring and bore wear, or warped cylinder heads.

If, when taking the potential purchase for a test drive, fumes enter the cabin, this could be a sign that the heat exchangers are worn or damaged. Check also that the sills, which contain the integral heater tubes, are not rotted or damaged. Ideally, heat exchangers should be replaced on a regular basis; although readily available, these are not cheap items. If a musty aroma is detected within the cabin it is almost certainly an indication of dampness

continued on page 81

GALLERY ··· GALLERY ··· GALLERY ··· GALLERY ··· GALLERY ···

The Karmann Ghia was launched on July 14, 1955, when it was well received. The French dubbed it poupée vivante: *'living doll'. (Courtesy National Motor Museum)*

Put into production in August 1957, the Convertible was unveiled at Frankfurt the following month. (Courtesy National Motor Museum)

GALLERY ··· GALLERY ··· GALLERY ··· GALLERY ··· GALLERY ···

The publicity material that Volkswagen used for the Karmann Ghia is particularly evocative of the 1950s and 1960s. The use of colour and the drawing techniques are typical of Ernst Reuters inasmuch as he exaggerated some of the car's lines. The sales patter featured on contemporary brochures, too, is representative of the period: 'In the extra quiet achieved by an absorptive roof lining. Made like a soundproof ceiling!' 'Truly, your only problem with a Karmann Ghia is to decide which model to buy ... Coupé or Convertible.' (Courtesy Volkswagen)

GALLERY ··· GALLERY ··· GALLERY ··· GALLERY ··· GALLERY ···

The Karmann Ghia Convertible was launched in August 1957, a month after production began. This brochure illustration shows that the model is every bit as elegant as the Coupé. (Courtesy National Motor Museum)

Good to look at; good to drive. The Karmann Ghia Convertible combined German thoroughness with Italian verve. (Courtesy National Motor Museum)

GALLERY ··· GALLERY ··· GALLERY ··· GALLERY ··· GALLERY ···

The Karmann Ghia's dashboard was never lavishly furnished; the fuel gauge was not a feature until after 1957. (Courtesy Martin McGarry)

The Karmann Ghia was well received in America: this is an American specification late Convertible model. (Courtesy Martin McGarry)

GALLERY ··· GALLERY ··· GALLERY ··· GALLERY ··· GALLERY ···

Volkswagen and Karmann publicity was among the most attractive, as this delightful postcard demonstrates. (Courtesy Volkswagen)

GALLERY ··· GALLERY ··· GALLERY ··· GALLERY ··· GALLERY ···

Despite superb styling and Volkswagen advertising which suggested the model was a true sports car, the Karmann Ghia cleverly enshrouded the Beetle's running gear. Whilst handling was more precise than that of the Beetle, and the aerodynamic shape gave a small improvement in top speed, acceleration did not match its streamlined shape. (Courtesy Volkswagen and Jenna Publishing)

GALLERY ··· GALLERY ··· GALLERY ··· GALLERY ··· GALLERY ···

Right: The Type 3's cabin was designed with comfort in mind, with a dashboard different to that of the Type 1: note the speaker grille on the fascia, it's designed to match the instruments. (Author's collection)

Karmann's stylish Type 3 in a desert setting that appeared in a Danish sales brochure of 1966. (Author's collection)

GALLERY ··· GALLERY ··· GALLERY ··· GALLERY ··· GALLERY ···

GALLERY ··· GALLERY ··· GALLERY ··· GALLERY ··· GALLERY ···

Another desert shot from the Dutch brochure really shows off the Type 1's stylishness. (Author's collection)

GALLERY ··· GALLERY ··· GALLERY ··· GALLERY ··· GALLERY ···

GALLERY··· GALLERY··· GALLERY··· GALLERY··· GALLERY···

Coupé

Now step back. Gaze upon her ... this Volkswagen Karmann Ghia. Eve
curvature of the body, the large contoured windows tell a story of grea
And a promise of roominess that comes true the minute you step inside
very first ride. And what a ride! Sure and steady, she handles with cons
notwithstanding. You see, both Coupé and Convertible have independe
four wheels, plus a stabilizer and hydraulic steering damper. And inside
masterpiece, you find cushioned contour seats ... sporty seats with a per
easily, individually, to suit your leg length, your most comfortable back
and enjoy complete driving pleasure ... for brief errands, for hours-long

GALLERY ❖ ❖ GALLERY ❖ ❖ GALLERY ❖ ❖ GAL

Who could fail to be impressed by this description of the Karmann Ghia's many qualities? (Courtesy National Motor Museum)

e says quality ... quietly. The easy
in design, in engineering.
comfort that delights you ... on your
te ease ... sharp turns
sion-bar suspension for all
uxuriously fabric-trimmed
ty all their own. They adjust
. Just relax

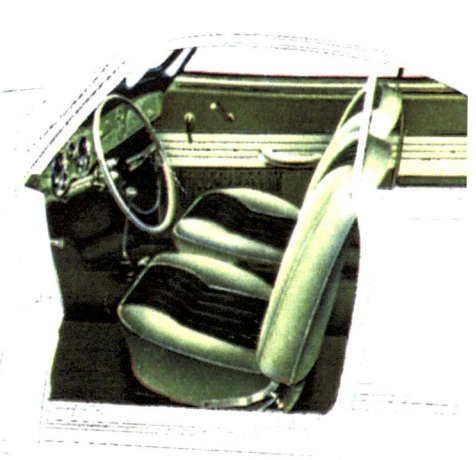

Do you like a car that's easy to enter? With nice wide doors...and "stops" that hold the door open at convenient angles? Karmann Ghia caters for your comfort.

GALLERY ··· GALLERY ··· GALLERY ··· GALLERY ··· GALLERY ···

Marrying chassis and body together. This car dates from approximately 1965-66. (Author's collection)

GALLERY ··· GALLERY ··· GALLERY ··· GALLERY ··· GALLERY ···

Last of the Karmann Ghias. Production of European specification models ceased at the end of December 1973. Production of American specification models this like continued at Osnabrück until June 21, 1974. (Author's collection)

GALLERY ··· GALLERY ··· GALLERY ··· GALLERY ··· GALLERY ···

The Karmann family 1970-71. The 1302LS Cabriolet is flanked by a Karmann Ghia Convertible and a Coupé. (Author's collection)

A late model Karmann Ghia Type 1 Coupé. (Courtesy VAG UK)

continued from page 64

and a full inspection under the carpets is advisable.

With the engine lid open, check for petrol leaks from the carburettor. Such leaks are dangerous and could be a fire hazard. The remedy is quite simple, requiring only a change of carburettor which can be easily obtained.

The gearbox is exceptionally rugged and should present few problems. If there is evidence that all is not well, do not attempt a DIY rebuild unless suitably qualified. Replacement gearboxes are plentiful and any repairs are best left to a Volkswagen specialist. Clutches, too, are built for longevity, can be easily replaced and are not overly expensive. A common cause of a slipping clutch is often a sticking cable and may not be attributed to the clutch mechanism at all. If it is necessary to replace the clutch there is no alternative but to remove the engine, a job which, on the Volkswagen, is much easier than most other cars.

Attempting restoration of a car in this condition is a job for the dedicated enthusiast only! (Courtesy Martin McGarry)

Some cars may appear beyond restoration ... (Courtesy Martin McGarry)

... but specialist attention can produce specialist results! (Courtesy Martin McGarry)

Some leakage of oil may be apparent through the gaiters on the inner section of the rear axle tubes; this need not be a major problem if the spillage is slight and the gearbox topped-up regularly. Heavy leakage, however, could lead to the gearbox running dry.

The Karmann Ghia's suspension, like that of the Beetle's, is rugged but that does not mean it is without problems. At worst, the suspension can sag which will mean it's time to carry out an overhaul. Dampers should also be checked at the same time as bearings and swivels; ensure king pins are satisfactory at the same time. The ball joints of later cars are less likely to wear than king pins, however. It may be found that a car's suspension has been lowered and, in such cases, the potential purchaser should be satisfied that the work has been carried out in accordance with specialist advice.

Quite conventional is the Karmann Ghia's braking system which is unlikely to present undue difficulties.

Trim components can be expensive - find a car with as many undamaged trim items as possible. (Courtesy Martin McGarry)

Expect normal wear and tear to occur: if the brake pedal has unusually long travel or fails to halt the car satisfactorily, suspect the seals of the master cylinder which will more than likely have split or perished. Early cars were fitted with single circuit master cylinders and it goes without saying that the dual circuit types as fitted to later cars are more complicated. Both types are reliable and can be readily obtained. Corroded brake pipes can prove hazardous so, while inspecting the system, check that the wheel cylinders are working correctly and are free from leaks.

The steering design on the Karmann Ghia has proved reliable and a car in good condition will enjoy a relatively light and precise feel. A little movement in the steering wheel can be expected but if this is excessive suspect wear in the steering joints. Like all things Volkswagen, the mechanisms are all repairable. Undue play in the trailing arms in relation to the axle beam will mean the bushes and bearings in the steering assembly require immediate attention. Wear in the steering box is normally confined to its centre position and it has been known for boxes to run dry.

Having chosen a particular car there are a number points to consider. Firstly, even if the car is in pristine condition and likely to attract attention at enthusiast events, do not expect it to be an investment as the overall numbers in existence will prevent the marque from becoming a cherished rarity. Consider the car's pedigree; nice to look at it may be but the Karmann Ghia does not have a history of motorsport and neither is it recognised for outstanding performance. Moreover, the car's mechanical design equates it firmly with other Beetle variants, complete with its relatively noisy drivetrain which loses points on sophistication, however reliable and strong it is.

For the purchaser who has opted for a vehicle that clearly is in need of care and attention, ahead there is a tortuous route to getting the car to the desired condition, requiring determination and a lot of patience. If choosing to buy a car from a specialist it will pay to first discuss the pending purchase in detail. This will help decide whether to purchase a car that has already been restored or to have a particular car imported. Whatever, make sure that a comprehensive guide is obtained of what is actually going to be provided and what the project will cost. Talking to Martin McGarry, the service he provides does appear to be very thorough and comprehensive; no doubt other reputable specialists will offer a similar service.

Not all enthusiasts want to carry out the restoration of a car themselves and will choose to entrust the work to a specialist. Before committing to any work it is important that both parties know what is required of each other.

When buying a car it will be useful to know as much of the car's history as possible; in the case of a car with UK registration, it's prudent to check whether it is known to any of the enthusiasts' clubs, the Karmann Ghia Owners' Club in particular.

Restoration - a brief guide

Much of the mechanical work involved in restoring a Karmann Ghia is so closely related to that of the Beetle it is not intended to reiterate what is already available to guide you through this particular task. The following is, therefore, provided to assist owners in the general restoration of the bodywork and is limited to that which can be carried out at home without the use of specialist tools and equipment. It is not a DIY guide but merely an overview of some of the procedures required in carrying out particular tasks. Unless thoroughly competent, all repair and replacement work should be left to a skilled specialist who will have the necessary experience and equipment to ensure a completely satisfactory result. On a car such as the Karmann Ghia, where exact tolerances are employed, any repair work on the body sections has to be carried out to a very high standard. A lack of knowledge in this respect can lead to extensive damage which may prove difficult to rectify.

BUMPERS, FRONT & REAR

Before starting to dismantle the front bumper, the spare wheel will have to be removed in order to locate the bumper brackets. These will be seen on each side of the spare wheel housing. Once these are removed the retaining bolts and brackets on the outer panel should be undone, which will allow the complete bumper assembly to be pulled away from the car.

Do not forget to remove the bumper bracket covers; unscrewing the two bolts either side of the bumper will enable the brackets and overriders to be detached. It will be seen that the two outer sections of the bumper can be dismantled; make sure that all grommets are removed and that the seals are in good order.

Installation is basically a reversal of the above procedure; bolt the outer sections to the bumper's centre portion, fix the bumper to the body by its brackets, making sure the whole assembly is uniform. Importantly, ensure that the covers for the bracket assembly are correctly sealed.

To remove the rear bumper the two bracket retaining bolts on either side should be undone, together with the single securing bolt on both sides; the bumper, including the overriders, should be pulled clear of the rear panel. Overriders and spacers can be removed from the bumper by undoing the single retaining bolts. The brackets can be removed also. Two further bolts will be found on the sides of the bumper itself and, by removing these, it is possible to detach the outer parts from the bumper centre portion.

As with the front bumper, re-assembly is completed in the reverse order, firstly checking the condition of the seals and replacing any that are damaged.

Removal and installation of American specification bumpers is different. Having removed the bolts from both brackets and the two outer sections, it should be possible to pull the whole bumper assembly away from the front panel. The overrider support nuts can be undone as well as the bracket covers. Once the bolts holding the outer part of the bumper are unscrewed, make sure all the grommets are removed from the front panel of the car. A check should be made to see whether any parts require renewal before refitting in the reverse order.

Removing American specification bumpers at the rear will initially involve undoing the two overrider support bolts on each side; before removing the bumper assembly complete, it is necessary to undo the two bracket bolts as well as the single outer securing bolt on both sides of the assembly. Bolts for the bow section and outer bumper sections can be clearly seen and should be undone to renovate any of the component parts. Installation is a reversal of the foregoing, ensuring fitment is uniform.

The procedure for Type 3 cars is naturally different. To remove the front bumper it is first necessary to undo the screws found in the left- and right-hand side panels, which will enable the bumper brackets to be detached. The bumper assembly can then be pulled away in its entirety. Once removed, the overriders and the outer sections of the bumper can be detached if necessary.

Removing the rear bumper is simple inasmuch as only the screws on the left and right quarter panels need be undone to lift the assembly away from the car; retaining brackets can then be detached. Installation is a reversal of the foregoing.

EXTERNAL TRIM

The exterior trim consists of three elements: fresh air inlets on the nose cone, front side panel mouldings and door trim mouldings.

The fresh air inlets are secured to the bodywork by three retaining screws; once removed a further three screws hold the grille and flyscreen in place. It may be necessary to replace the rubber seal and, if the grille is damaged, this may have to be replaced as well.

Front side panel trim mouldings

Door hinges are secured by four Phillips screws. Note that the interior of this car has been completely stripped during restoration. (Courtesy Martin McGarry)

Floorpan repairs, like this, will be a common requirement. (Courtesy Martin McGarry)

are clipped to the bodywork and can be pushed out from the inside. When re-fitting, it is advisable to use a suitable sealant.

To remove door trim mouldings it is necessary to remove both the window winder and inner door handle. This will allow access to the door panel and the plastic sheet behind it. The moulding clips will be visible and can be pushed out. When re-fitting ensure a sealant is used to secure the clips.

INTERIOR TRIM

This is much more complex than the external trim and comprises the lining to the luggage compartment, cabin headlining, front and quarter panel linings. Also included are carpets, glove compartment, parcel shelf and dashboard cover.

The interior luggage compartment lining can only be removed with the rear seat squab folded; underneath the lining will be found sound absorbing material which may require replacement. Make sure all traces of the original adhesive are removed before any remedial work is carried out.

To remove the headlining (Coupé) satisfactorily it will be necessary to take out the windscreen, quarterlights and rear window. The weatherstrip moulding around the doors will also have to be removed, as will that for the quarterlights. Next, remove the rear-view mirror, and dismantle the interior light. The headlining can then be carefully removed.

The lining on the quarter panels can quite simply be pulled from position once the rear seat back has been folded. The two countersunk screws should be removed as well. The moulded trim can also be detached by bending the retaining lugs upward.

Front panel linings can be similarly removed; it is important that all traces of cement from inside the body are cleaned off before re-fitting with a suitable adhesive. Both side member carpets can be taken away at this point, but take care to undo all eight screws holding the scuff plate in position. Before replacing the carpet trim use an adhesive and place a sealing strip under the scuff plate. The rear end of the carpet can be secured with a carpet tack.

In removing the rear parcel shelf it will be necessary to take out the rear window and detach the rear seat squab hooks; remove also the retaining plate for the warm air outlet. The shelf trim moulding should be removed, the shelf covering gently pulled away and any traces of old adhesive cleaned off. If a new shelf is installed make sure a cut-out is made for the warm air outlet.

The windscreen will have to be removed when dismantling the instrument panel cover, as will the fireboard covering for the luggage compartment. The glovebox should also be removed, together with the passenger grab handle and speaker grille. Take care to undo the two screws on each warm air vent.

To remove the glovebox first open the luggage compartment and take out the fireboard panel. The glovebox can now be pulled away once the retaining strap has been unscrewed, and the glovebox lid detached by unscrewing the two hinge screws. To change the glovebox lock use a pair of circlip pliers. When re-fitting the glovebox be careful to tighten the retaining strap.

Having taken out and replaced the rear quarterlights there can be a tendency for water leaks in various places. The main points where this is likely are: 1) the bottom of the channel between the quarterlights and door windows; 2) the bottom of the quarterlight weatherstrip; 3) the lower window weatherstrip at the rear end of the trim moulding; 4) the channel between the vertical weatherstrip between the quarterlight and door window, and 5) the joint where the door window weatherstrip on the roof frame meets the quarterlight and door windows. Remedies to the foregoing are: 1) use a sealant to seal the angle weatherstrip; 2) having removed the window use a plastic sealer to fill the joint between the weatherstrip and the channel. Cover with a sealing compound. It may be necessary to adjust the upper end of the beading by approximately 2 inches (50mm) so that it cannot absorb moisture; 3) by removing the rear window and weatherstrip to include the retaining channel; all old adhesive should be cleaned off. If there is any excess of headlining at this point it should be trimmed so that no moisture is trapped; 4) use a suitable cement to bond the vertical weatherstrip; 5) use plastic filler to fill the joint between the channel and door window weatherstrip. The upper weatherstrip should be joined to the door window weatherstrip with a suitable adhesive.

The interior trim of Type 3 cars is installed in a similar way to that of Type 1 cars. The instrument panel cover is easier to remove and all that is necessary is to remove the six retaining nuts from the underside using a T-wrench to undo them from the cover studs. The moulding on the lower part of the fascia is easily removed once the ashtray is detached and the nuts undone from the moulding strip fastened behind the instrument panel. The glovebox assembly can be undone by unscrewing the striker plate screws and taking off the striker plate itself. The lower securing nut can then be removed and the glovebox lifted out in a downward movement. It is important to note that, as from chassis number 0 042 251 (May 1962), the steering wheel was altered in height by 20mm, which called for a slightly redesigned lower cover for the instrument panel.

Doors, windows & seats

To remove a door, look for the door-check spring mounting. Two retaining screws will be seen and these must be removed. Each door hinge is secured by four crosshead-type screws. Using a punch screwdriver, loosen these and then completely undo them with a crosshead screwdriver. The doors can now be removed.

When replacing a door, offer it up so that it aligns completely; the hinges are screwed to adjustable plates to allow correct fitting.

Make sure that any weatherstrip which shows signs of wear, or is damaged, is replaced using the correct adhesive. Adjust the striker plate, checking that the rubber buffers are in good order and, if required, replace. Oil the hinges and note that the material used for the hinges was changed to a light metal from chassis number 2 395 181 (28.4.59), and that hinge pins have plastic bushes. Lubricate the door locks with powdered graphite only.

The windows have three means of adjustment: vertical, longitudinal and sideways. To adjust vertically firstly remove the inner panel together with the window winder, door handle and plastic sheet. The adjusting screws can now be seen and it will be possible to slacken the lock nut. The adjusting screws can be turned either to the left - to lower the glass - or right - to raise it. By closing the door it can be seen whether the glass is at the right height; when correct, tighten the adjusting lock nut.

Plastic buffers assist in controlling the glass in the window slot; should the four buffers be proud the glass can become marked, which is preceded by a rubbing noise. It is important that the buffers work uniformly and these can be simply adjusted by introducing a thin wedge to compress the buffers if the contact is too great. Alternatively, use a piece of metal, bent to form a hook, to pull the buffers nearer the glass.

To adjust longitudinally it should be checked that the weatherstrip moulding between the door and the quarterlight is both secure and straight. It may be necessary to remove the weatherstrip and coat the inside with an adhesive before refitting. The play between the window lift runners may be excessive, which can be rectified by squeezing the runners together with a pair of pliers. Ensure that the clearance between the glass and the weatherstrip is uniform. Should this not rectify the problem it will be necessary to undo the four hexagonal screws on the window lift channel; adjust the channel accordingly and tighten the securing screws.

To correct side adjustment it may be necessary to loosen the top retaining screws of the window roller bracket. This should be done with the window fully raised and the bracket pressed against the roller; the screws can then be tightened. For further adjustment slacken the hexagon head and countersunk screws of the window guide rail; to obtain the correct window position turn the three screw pins at the top and bottom of the guide rail either in or out. Tighten both the hexagonal and countersunk screws once the adjustment of the glass is correct, the weatherstrip in the roof and quarterlight provide the location points.

In order to remove the windscreen, the wipers and wiper arms have first to be detached. It is then a question of pushing the weatherstrip and window from inside the car, starting from the passenger side. (There's no other reason for starting on the passenger's side than that there is more space).

When installing a new windscreen, start by placing the weatherstrip with its joint at the top-centre of the screen. The task of actually fitting the screen is made all the easier if two people do it. By inserting a cord around the screen moulding, the trim can then be placed into position so that the cord ends hang on the inside edge of the glass. With one person offering the screen from the outside, and the other pulling from the inside, the screen can be fitted in place. The rear screen can be removed and refitted following a similar procedure.

When fitting rear quarterlights all existing trim and adhesive should be thoroughly cleaned away; a plastic sealer can then be forced into the retaining channel and the new moulding placed into position. The glass can then be slid into position and tapped home with a rubber hammer if necessary. When the fit is good the window trim can be screwed into place.

For cars with opening rear quarterlights, the window should be in the open position; the toggle retaining screws can then be undone and the weatherstrip pulled away from the door panel. Three countersunk screws will be located on the door panel and, with these removed, it will be possible to remove the window in its entirety. Repairs and replacements to the window trim can be made before the window is re-installed.

Seats on the Karmann Ghia can be readily removed. The locking mechanism on the right-hand side of the seat should be lifted and the seat pushed forward and clear of the guide rails. It is a good idea to grease the guide rails before refitting the seat.

Replacement body sections
Roof replacement
The roof on the Karmann Ghia Coupé is normally not an area prone to rot. However, should a roof need to be replaced, this is obviously a major undertaking. In replacing the roof it is necessary to disconnect the battery and remove all interior trim to include the rear-view mirror and sun visors.

It might be prudent to remove the seats, but this is a matter of choice. If left in position ensure that they are adequately protected.

The windscreen will have to be removed, together with the rear screen and quarterlights. Door windows should be wound fully down and the glass slots well protected. Care should be taken to protect the dashboard; remove the steering wheel and the windscreen wipers, and fully cover all exposed parts of the car.

The existing welds on the roof pillars would normally have to be heated with a weld torch before being scraped away until it is possible to detach the roof in its entirety. The cuts are made at something like 2 inches (50mm) above the weld seams. All remaining metal can then be removed as far as the welds, ensuring that the metal is clean and welds ground down and filled as necessary. Any cosmetic work should be carried out at this stage. The replacement roof can then be positioned, having already ensured that the inner panels of the pillars are not distorted. This is important as these serve as overlap joints.

The specialist will have a series of window gauges which will provide the essential measurements. With the gauges in place, the roof is put into position and tack-welds made to the front scuttle. The rear pillars are also tack-welded into position. Gas welding is used on the roof pillars inside and out, before the weld seams are ground as far as practicable. Once complete, the weld areas can be filled and smoothed and the joints ground to a smooth finish and prepared for painting.

There may be instances where it is desirable for single pillars to be removed and replaced. In general, the procedure is the same as for a full roof removal. Roof pillars can be sawn off 2 inches (50mm) above the lower weld seam and at the same distance below the upper weld seam. The new pillar can be put into position and welded accordingly.

Front side panels
In preparing for this task it is essential to remove the front bumper, luggage compartment lid, doors, front wheels, spare wheel, hinge cover plate in the spare wheel housing and the weatherstrip on the luggage compartment surround. It is also necessary to disconnect the battery, together with all electrical accessories, including headlamps.

Where accident damage has occurred it would normally be necessary to replace the hinge pillar gusset plate. Complete hinge pillar replacement, however, would not be advisable unless the roof is being replaced. With the roof *in situ* it should only be necessary to cut the hinge pillar at the bottom of the roof pillar to allow the new section, which will have been cut to fit, to be butt-welded into place. Debris should be removed and spot-welding marks ground flat.

With the gusset plate clamped in position, welding can take place, folding over the gusset plate outer edge. The door can then be installed, after checking all clearances and allowing between 8-10mm (0.50inch) between the door and the gusset plate over its entire length. With the clearances satisfactory, the door can be removed to allow fitting and assembly of the side panel. Only when the fit is perfect is it possible to weld; initially tack-welds should be made to the sill panel, windscreen frame joints and the front panel, as well as along the opening of the luggage compartment.

Several checks are normally required to ensure correct fit and only when completely satisfactory should the outer edge of the side panel be folded over and welded to the gusset plate. Once the lower edge of the side panel has been welded to the hinge pillar, and the headlamp assembly installed, all the weld joints can be smoothed out and made ready for painting.

REAR QUARTER PANELS

Rear quarter panels comprise several components: outer quarter panel, inner quarter panel (which is attached to the quarter window area) and inner and outer wheel housings.

As a means of installation, the

Although not too clear in this photo, the area above the air intake is rusting badly and bubbling the paint. A further area of serious corrosion can be seen to the left of the indicator light aperture. (Courtesy Martin McGarry)

quarter panel on the Coupé should be spot-welded to the lower pillar; in addition to the inner quarter panel being attached to the quarterlight area, it is also welded to the inner wheel housing, the quarter panel, lock and roof pillars. At its lower points the quarter panel is spot-welded to the outer wheel housing and rear side panel. As the inner and outer wheel housings are separate items, these can be replaced independently.

The bodywork procedure for replacing the rear quarter panels is a complicated business and should only be undertaken by a professional with specific skills.

The relevant repair work on the Type 3 is similarly specialist and should not be undertaken without the necessary experience.

Luggage & engine compartment lids

It may be necessary on occasion to remove and refit the luggage and engine compartment lids. The luggage compartment lid is particularly cumbersome and it is recommended that two people do the job in order to reduce the likelihood of damaging either it or the bodywork. On both Type 1 and Type 3 cars, retaining bolts support the hinges at each side of the lid; once these are undone the lid can be removed. Although installation is a complete reversal of dismantling, check the condition of the weatherstrip and, if necessary, replace. Take care when replacing the weatherstrip that all adhesive debris is cleaned off.

If it is necessary to repair or replace the locking mechanism, the retaining spring will have to be unhooked. By removing the lining of the luggage compartment the hinge securing bolts can be located and undone. By undoing the lock cable clamp screw, the locking cable can be removed from the catch and the lock removed.

The engine compartment lid is similarly straightforward to remove. With the lid open the registration plate lamp cable can be unclipped and pulled out of the clamping plate. The lid's two hinges are retained by two bolts each and once these are removed the lid itself can be detached.

To re-install the lid the weatherstrip must first be checked and replaced if necessary. If a new weatherstrip is needed ensure first that the surface is clean and free from adhesive. If dismantling the lock it will be necessary to unscrew the lock bolt and remove the four retaining bolts; the clamp screw can be loosened and the cable and lock removed. The cable can be withdrawn via the pull-knob inside the car. Re-installation of the assembly calls for greasing of the lock cable mechanism.

Problems with the sun roof

By its nature the sun roof (when fitted to Type 1 cars and electrically operated on Type 3 cars) is exposed to all the elements and water which enters the roof-opening runs along drainage channels in the sliding roof frame. Passing through pipes and hoses in the front roof pillar, the water drains to the front of the car. Excess water, which drains at the rear of the sun roof assembly, is channelled out of the two drain slots in the roof at the back.

To clear blocked drain hoses a compressed air line should be used; alternatively, feed a flexible wire from underneath the car. If drain hoses are to be refitted, always make sure they are not kinked or trapped.

On Type 3 cars, the electric motor and drive gear are accessed from the rear of the headlining and are concealed by a zip-fastening.

Should the electrical system for the sliding panel fail, the roof can be operated with a handle, which would have been supplied with the vehicle from new. By inserting the handle into the drive mechanism - first removing a plastic cap fastened by a Phillips screw - the panel can be opened or closed.

The drive gear can be removed from the roof assembly by firstly undoing the retaining screws; the roof's side runners and cables can also be removed by undoing the five screws from the side and corner runners on each side of the panel. Once the corner runners have been taken out it should be possible to pull the side runners - complete with cables and trim panel - out of the opening. Extreme care should of course be taken not to damage the paintwork.

Installing a sliding roof is a job that requires a lot of patience. The first task is to insert the sliding roof trim panel into the guide grooves, pushing it back as far as possible; this should be done before securing any of the side runners. The cables should be checked for wear and replacements fitted if necessary. It is important to check that both cables have equal wear otherwise the roof will not align. When lubricating cables, ensure that only molybdenum-disulphide grease is used before sliding the cables into the guide tubes. With the corner and side runners installed, the sliding roof panel should be fitted and the drive gear installed. The cables can then be connected to the motor.

There may be occasions when adjustments have to be made with the roof *in situ*. To adjust the cables the

First registered in the UK on March 1 1972 (CAX 444), this Coupé underwent considerable refurbishment between 1990 and 1991, which included fitting a reconditioned 1600 engine. (Courtesy Martin McGarry)

roof has to be in the closed position before the cables can be disconnected from the drive gear, which can then be removed. The two rear guides can be pulled with the cables as far as the sliding roof supports; the rear guide brackets can be inserted into the supports while in the upright position and the drive gear installed before connection of the cables to the motor. Making sure that the drive gear engages the cables, operate the sliding roof mechanism several times.

The sliding panel can also be adjusted to achieve the correct height: after detaching the trim panel and pushing it back as far as it will go, the screws can be loosened from the front guide rails and knurled knobs turned to adjust the front of the roof to the correct level. On re-assembly, the screws should be tightened on the guide rails. At the rear of the roof a nut can be loosened on the upper pins and a screw on the bracket adjusted to obtain the desired height. When achieved, the loosened nut should be re-tightened. After checking that the roof operates correctly, the trim panel can be re-assembled.

Should the sliding roof lift on one side only it may be because the lifting mechanism is not running on its ramp because the ramps are not correctly aligned. The ramps should be located longitudinally so that, as the front panel edge comes into contact with the front seal, the brackets are at an angle of 45 degrees. To alter the lifter contact point slightly, the ramps should be tapped either backwards or forwards as required. If the cables on the drive gear are damaged, either or both must be replaced. The brackets may be set too low and, if this is the case, should be adjusted accordingly.

Problems can occur with the roof not sliding in a parallel fashion; if the side adjustment is incorrect the cables or height mechanism will have to be aligned. It goes without saying that, should the cables or drive gear be damaged, replacement parts will have to be fitted.

Is a DIY rebuild worth the effort? Ask those enthusiasts who have taken the plunge and now drive very desirable and reliable cars. It is an experience never to be forgotten - their Karmann Ghias are proof of that. Although a DIY rebuild is a complex operation and one not to be taken lightly, it can be done - and to award-winning standards, too.

Customising cars often involves lowering suspension and stripping the car of all its bright work. In this case even the 'nostrils' have disappeared, as well as the bumpers. Of course, not all Karmann Ghia enthusiasts agree with this type of treatment ... (Courtesy Martin McGarry)

Customising - and going faster

However pretty and desirable the Karmann Ghia is, there is definitely room for improvement when it comes to power output.

The Karmann Ghia's relative sedateness gave rise to the availability of tuning kits - but never from Volkswagen. Okrasa was possibly the foremost name; a pair of Solex carburettors and twin-port cylinder heads increased the compression ratio to 7.5:1, providing a 30 per cent increase in power from the 30bhp motor. Increased power could also be achieved by swapping the engine and gearbox for that of a 356 Porsche - but at an extortionate price!

In motorsport terms the Karmann Ghia was never a serious contender, and its only claim to fame was the private entry of a Type 3 for the 1965 Monte Carlo Rally. Apart from this, sadly, the marque was absent from track and rally events.

With the appropriate conversion kit the 34bhp engine could be made to deliver punchy performance using larger pistons and barrels. Top speeds of not far off 100mph (160km/h) make the Karmann Ghia a desirable machine.

Superchargers - of which the Judson was amongst the favourites - enjoyed a spell of popularity and transformed the output of a 1200cc engine into that which a 1600cc engine could offer.

Customising now means replacing the original seats with designer products and furnishing the car's interior trim with exotic materials to make it all the more plush. Suspension is lowered to give the Karmann Ghia a more aggressive appearance and alloy wheels help complete the image. Sometimes the car is stripped of all its bright external trim, and that includes the bumpers.

Exactly how far the performance of a Karmann Ghia can be uprated is relative to how much is spent. If buying a Karmann Ghia with the intent of 'hotting up' its performance, it would be sensible to buy a late model with twin-port engine. Possibly the first task would be to replace the car's exhaust system with one available from a tuning specialist. This will substantially pep up the car's momentum. Replacing the carburettor with a twin-choke variety will provide even more push.

For the Karmann Ghia owner who wants more in the way of performance for what is essentially an everyday car, it's not advisable to push the power output more than 15bhp above the norm. Anything much more than this will require specialist attention and considerable expense.

When this Coupé was manufactured, production of the Karmann Ghia was almost at an end. At Osnabrück the assembly lines were being converted for production of the VW Scirocco. The Eurobumpers depicted on this vehicle are tell-tale features of late cars. (Courtesy Martin McGarry)

In the power stakes the Karmann Ghia is certainly now in the performance league, thanks to a dedicated team of drag-race enthusiasts. Fitted with a 2-litre engine, the Karmann-Addiction racer certainly has the potential to leave scorch marks on the tarmac!

As interest in the Karmann Ghia grows there is less chance of cars being unnecessarily broken up. The car is unique inasmuch that its numbers - as far as the United Kingdom is concerned - are actually increasing, as a result of a steady number of cars being rescued and imported from America. The Karmann Ghia Owners' Club has approximately 600-800 members who, between them, care for as many as 1000 cars. To enthusiasts worldwide, the sight and sound of a splendid Karmann Ghia is sweet indeed.

Coupés in such fine condition as this 1968 RHD car, owned by Chris Spencer and pictured in the English Lake District, make for an ideal classic car. When Chris bought the car it was in a sorry state, the total restoration taking some fifteen months to complete. (Author)

APPENDIX 1
PRODUCTION FIGURES

YEAR	TYPE 1 COUPÉ	TYPE 1 CONVERTIBLE	TYPE 3
1955	1282		
1956	11,555		
1957	15,369	105	
1958	14,515	4392	
1959	17,196	4585	
1960	19,259	5465	
1961	16,708	3965	661
1962	18,812	4570	8541
1963	22,829	5433	6720
1964	25,267	5262	7367
1965	28,387	5326	6873
1966	23,387	5395	5947
1967	19,406	4183	2819
1968	24,729	5713	2533
1969	27,834	6504	1049
1970	24,893	6398	
1971	21,133	6565	
1972	12,434	2910	
1973	10,462	2555	
1974	7167		
TOTAL	363,401	80,899	42,498

BRAZILIAN PRODUCTION

1962 759
1963 1868
1964 2285
1965 1951
1966 2400
1967 3009
1968 5000
1969 3459
1970 3107
1971 8011
1972 7130
1973 5788
1974 4947
1975 2099
1976 87

TOTAL 51,900

TOTAL PRODUCTION, GERMAN AND BRAZILIAN, OF ALL KARMANN GHIAS 538,698

APPENDIX 2
ORIGINAL SPECIFICATIONS

Karmann Ghia Type numbers

141	LHD Type 1 Convertible
142	RHD Type 1 Convertible
143	LHD Type 1 Coupé
144	RHD Type 1 Coupé
343	LHD Type 3 Coupé
344	RHD Type 3 Coupé
345	LHD Type 3 Coupé with electric sunroof
346	RHD Type 3 Coupé with electric sunroof

Karmann Ghia Type 1 (original specification)

ENGINE
Flat-four, ohv. air-cooled. Alloy crankcase and cylinder heads, cast iron barrels. 4 main bearings. Bore/stroke 77mm/64mm, 1192cc. Compression ratio 6.6:1. Mechanical fuel pump, Solex 28 PCI carburettor. Maximum power: 30bhp @ 3400 rpm.

TRANSMISSION
4-speed gearbox, synchromesh on 2nd, 3rd, and 4th ratios. Gear ratios: 1st 3.60; 2nd 1.88; 3rd 1.23; 4th 0.82; reverse 4.53; final drive 4.43:1. Clutch: single dry plate.

BRAKES
9inch (230mm) drums all round; hydraulic. Parking brake operating on rear drums.

SUSPENSION
Transverse torsion bars at front with twin trailing arms and double-acting shock absorbers and anti-roll bar. Transverse torsion bars at rear, trailing arms and swing axles; double-acting shock absorbers.

STEERING
Worm and nut, 2.4 turns lock-to-lock.

WHEELS AND TYRES
5.60 x 15 cross-ply.

DIMENSIONS
Wheelbase 94.5ins (2400mm);
Overall length 163ins (4140mm)
Overall width 64.2ins (1630mm)
Height 52.2ins (1325mm)
Dry weight .... 1742 lbs (790 kg)
Kerb weight .... 2448 lbs (1110 kg)

PERFORMANCE
Top speed 76mph (121.6km/h)
0-60 mph (96km/h) .... 28 seconds
Maximum speed in each gear:
1st 20mph (32km/h)
2nd 38mph (60.8km/h)
3rd 63mph (100.8km/h)

Karmann Ghia Type 3 (original specification)
ENGINE
Flat-four, ohv. air-cooled. Alloy crankcase and cylinder heads, cast iron barrels. 4 main bearings. Bore/stroke 83mm/69mm, 1493cc. Compression ratio 7.8:1. Mechanical fuel pump, Solex 32 PHN-1 carburettor. Maximum power: 45bhp @ 3800 rpm.

TRANSMISSION
4-speed gearbox, synchromesh on 2nd, 3rd and 4th ratios. Gear ratios: 1st 3.80; 2nd 2.06; 3rd 1.32; 4th 0.89; reverse 3.88; final drive 4.125:1. Clutch: single dry plate.

BRAKES
9.8 inch (250mm) drums all round; hydraulic. Parking brake operating on rear drums.

SUSPENSION
Transverse torsion bars at front with twin trailing arms and double-acting shock absorbers and anti-roll bar. Transverse torsion bars at rear, trailing arms and swing axles; double-acting shock absorbers.

STEERING
Worm and nut, 2.4 turns lock-to-lock.

WHEELS AND TYRES
6.00 x 15 cross-ply.

DIMENSIONS
Wheelbase..94.5ins (2400mm);
Overall length 168.5ins (4280mm)
Overall width 63.8ins (1620mm)
Height..52.6ins (1335mm)
Dry weight 2006lbs (910kg)
Kerb weight..2889lbs (1310kg)

PERFORMANCE
Top speed 82mph (131.2km/h)
0-60mph (96km/h) ....21 seconds
Maximum speed in each gear:
1st..30mph (48km/h)
2nd...49mph (78.4km/h)
3rd 68mph (108.8km/h)

ENGINE SPECIFICATIONS - LATER MODELS

Karmann Ghia	1300	1500	1600
Capacity (cc)	1285	1493	1584
Bore/	77mm	83mm	85.5mm
Stroke	69mm	69mm	69
Comp ratio	6.6:1 7.3:1 (high)	7.5:1	6.6:1 7.7:1, 7.5:1 (4.68 on)
Output	40bhp @ 4000rpm	53bhp @ 4200rpm	55bhp @ 4000rpm
Max speed	82.9mph 132.64km/h	82mph 131.2km/h	86mph 137.6km/h

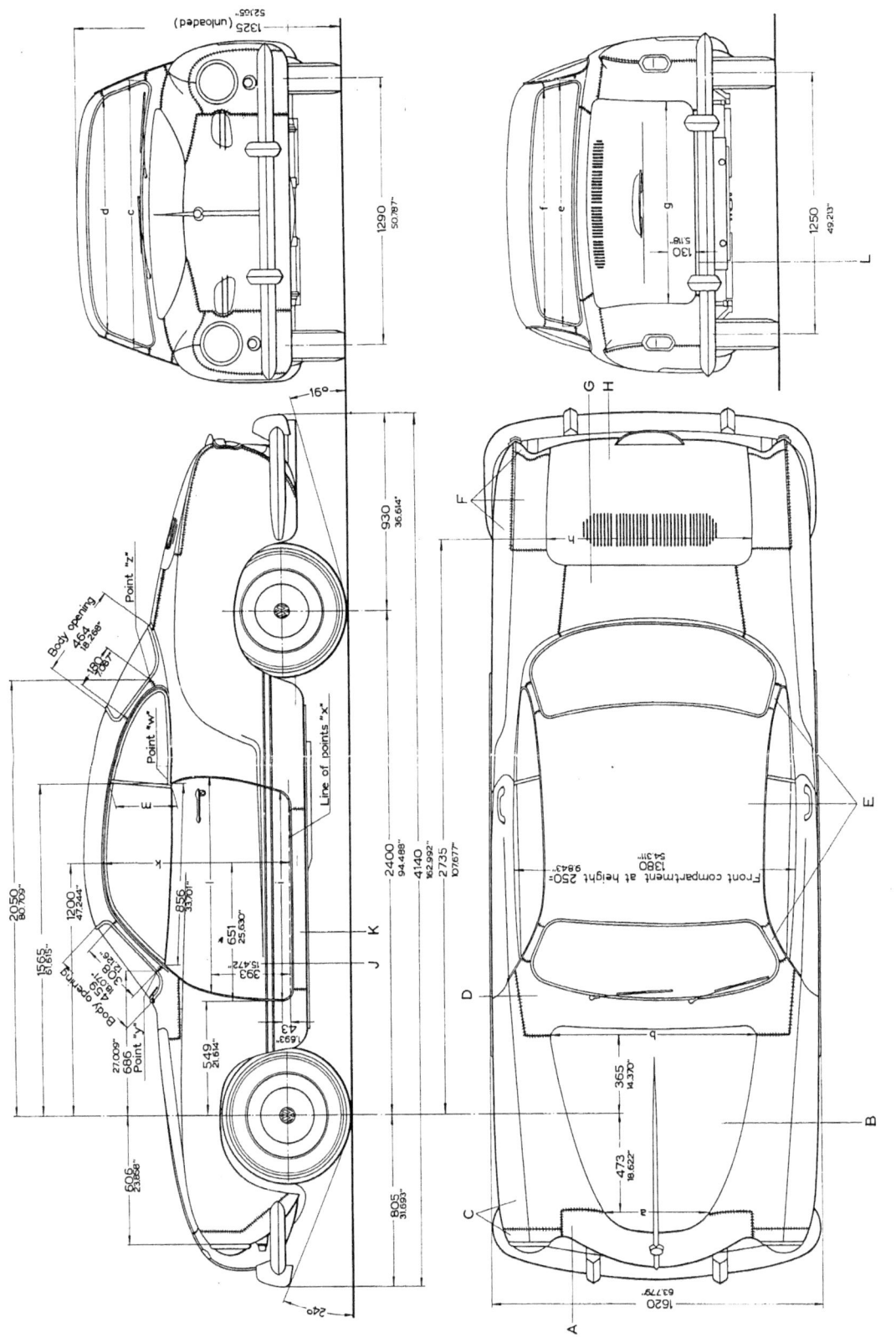

Early Type 1 Coupé. Plan and elevations with useful dimensional details. Major panel joints are also shown. Please ignore alphabetical references. *(Courtesy Karmann Ghia Owners' Club)*

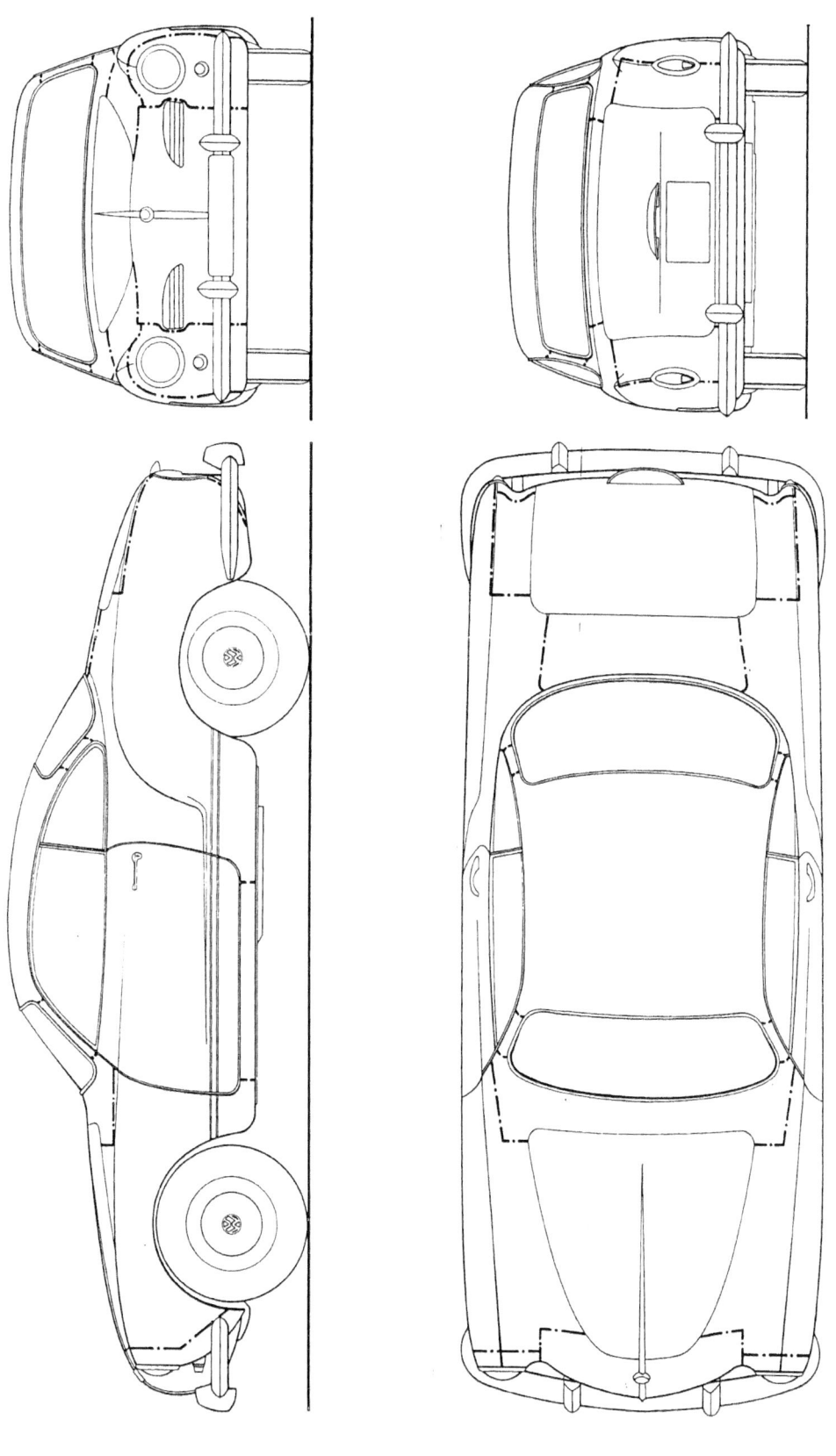

Later Type 1 Coupé in plan and elevation comprises the following major parts when welded together: front section outer panel, inner wheel housings, reinforcement plate, instrument panel and hinge pillars, rear luggage compartment floor plate, rear quarter panels with wheel housings, side members, roof, front and rear panels. (*Courtesy Karmann Ghia Owners' Club*)

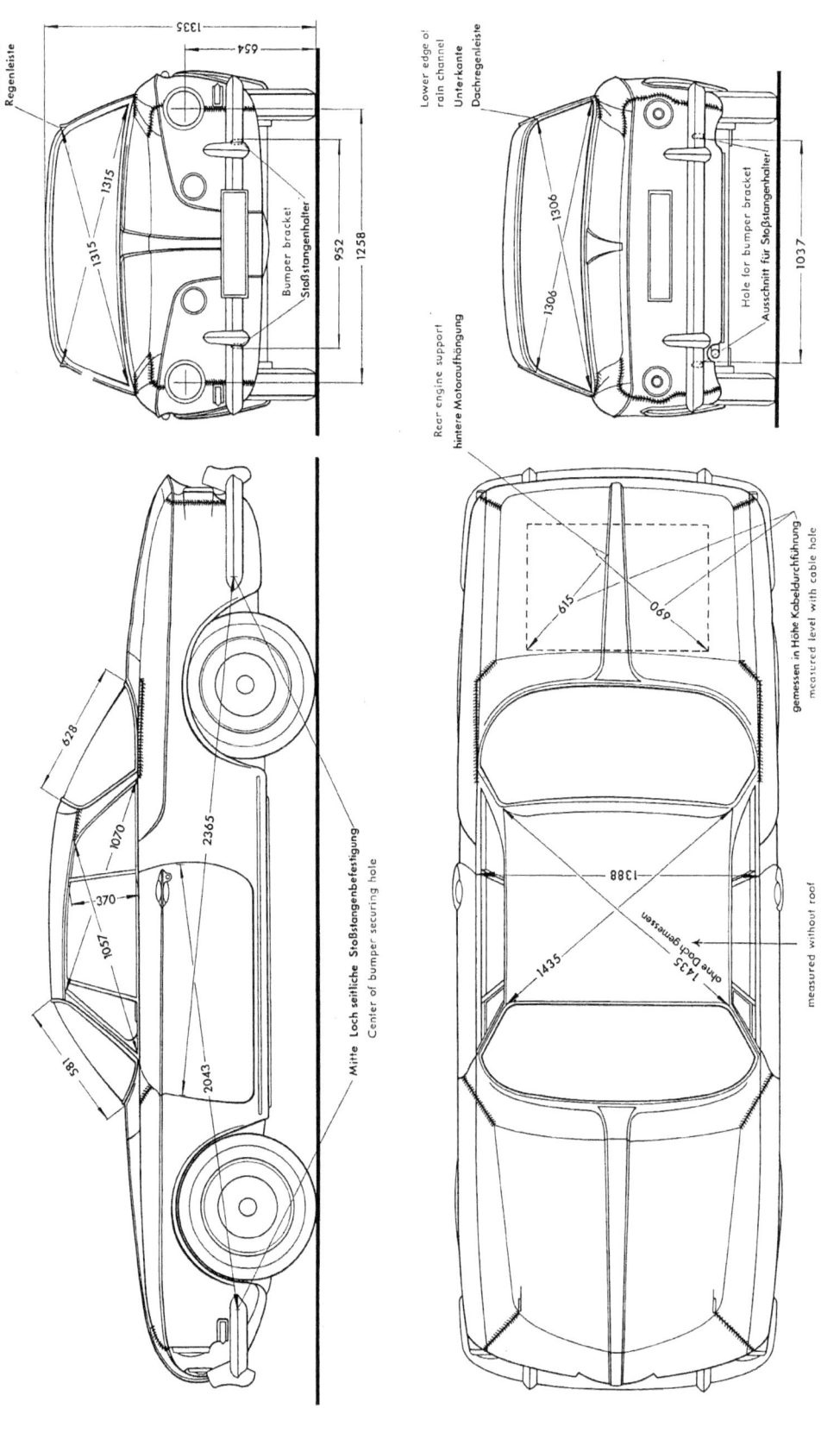

Type 3 Coupé in plan and elevation. The dimensions shown establish the correct relative positions of panels and exterior fittings. major panel joints are also shown. The body is comprised of the following parts welded together: front panel, reinforcement plate, instrument panel, front partition and hinge pillars (body front end), front side panels and wheel housings, quarter panels, wheel housings and luggage compartment floor (body rear end), outer panels, wings and roof. (*Courtesy Karmann Ghia Owners' club*)

APPENDIX 3
COLOURS

COLOUR	NUMBER	YEAR	TYPE 1	TYPE 3
Texas Brown	L271	54-55; 65-69	*	*
Kalahari Beige	L343	59-60	*	*
Cognac	L352	58	*	
Ferrite Brown	L453	65-77	*	
Silver Beige	L466	58-66	*	*
Sierra Beige	L490	62	*	
Sea Sand	L568	64-66	*	*
Earth Brown	L571	63	*	
Black	L41	7.49 on	*	*
Toucan Black	-	58	*	*
Capri Blue	L335	58-60	*	
Dolphin Blue	L337	58	*	
Sea Blue	L360	60-71	*	*
Arctis	L363	59-60	*	
Lavender	L397	62-72	*	
Pacific Blue	L398	60-71	*	
Bernina	L431	58	*	
Fjord Blue	L434	59-60	*	
Polar Blue	L532	63-71	*	
Iris Blue	-	56		*
Diamond Grey	L243	58-69	*	
Aero Silver	L228	58	*	
Seagull Grey	L347	59-61	*	
Dolphin Grey	L337	65-71	*	

COLOUR	NUMBER	YEAR	TYPE 1	TYPE 3
Graphite Silver	L428	58	*(Convertible)	
Basalt Grey	L467	58-64	*	
Anthracite	L469	62-77	*	*
Beige Grey	L472	56-71	*	*
Smoke Grey	L594	65-77	*	*
Fontana Grey	L595	65-77	*	*
Reseda Green	L14	55	*	
Mignotte Green	L14	59	*	
Bamboo	L241	58-59	*	
Mango Green	L346	59-2/61	*	
Pampass Green	L384	61-62	*	
Malachit Green	L444	65-71	*	
Emerald Green	L514	62	*	
Java Green	L518	64-67		*
Roulette Green	L554	64-71	*	*
Amazon	-	58	*	
Sealingwax Red	L53	50-65	*	*
Brilliant Red	L353	58	*	
Cardinal Red	L354	58	*	
India Red	L451	54-55, 60	*	
Paprika Red	L452	60-62	*	
Ruby Red	L456	61-67	*	*
Henna Red	L553	64-71	*	*
Cherry Red	L554	64-71	*	*
Colorado	-	58	*	
Granite Red	-	60	*	
Pearl White	L87	58-67	*(Convertible)	
Lotus White	L282	65-71	*	
Manilla Yellow	L560	62, 65-71	*	

APPENDIX 4
AT-A-GLANCE
CHRONOLOGY

1955	Karmann Ghia Coupé launched.
1956	Tubeless tyres adopted.
1957	Karmann Ghia Convertible launched.
1958	Fuel gauge fitted, Karmann Ghia.
1959	RHD Karmann-Ghia launched, 142/144. New front shape.
1960	40bhp engine. Full synchromesh on Karmann Ghia.
1961	Type 3 Karmann Ghia (343) launched.
1962	Improved brakes. Type 3 345 launched.
1964	Larger windows. RHD Type 3 344/346 launched.
1965	1300cc engine fitted.
1966	1500cc engine fitted.
1968	Double-jointed rear axles.
1969	New indicators. Type 3 production ends.
1970	1600cc engine fitted.
1971	New trim.
1973	Production ends, Karmann Ghia Convertible.
1974	Production ends, Karmann Ghia Coupé.

APPENDIX 5
SPECIALISTS, SUPPLIERS, CLUBS AND BIBLIOGRAPHY

Specialists & suppliers

Alan Schofield
Unit 14 Dinting Lane Industrial Estate
Glossop
Derbyshire, SK13 7NU
Tel: 01457 854267
Fax: 01457 860713
Web: www.alanschofield.com
Email: sales@alanschofield.com

Autocavan
103 Lower Weybourne Lane
Badshotlea
Farnham
Surrey
England
Tel: 01252 333891
Fax: 01252 343363
Parts. Contact company for branch addresses.

Beetlebugs VW
Unit D7 Acre Business Park
Acre Road
Reading
Berks RG2 05A
England
Tel: Freephone 0800 074 3604
Tel: 01344 466760
Fax: 0118 978 5595
Web: www.beetlebugs.co.uk
Email: enquiries@beetlebugs.co.uk
Conversions, sales & service.

Beetlelink
Unit D2 Preymead Farm
Badshot Lea
Farnham
Surrey GU9 9UT
England
Tel: 01252 326767
Parts, repairs, servicing and sales.

Bughaus
Colwick Road
Nottingham, NG2 4BG
Tel: 0115 958 9265
Web: www.bughaus.co.uk

Californian Classics
Unit 3 Ridge West Industrial Estate
St Leonard's on Sea
East Sussex, TN37 7PJ
Tel: 01424 752217, 07527 232940
Web: www.californianclassics.co.uk
Imports (viewing by appointment only)

Continental Auto Spares
64 Haxby Road
York
England
Tel: 01904 610286
Tel: 01904 633060 (workshop)
Parts and repairs.

Custom & Commercial
Unit 11, Bookham Industrial Estate
Church Road
Bookham
Surrey, KT23 3EU
Tel: 01372 452622, 01372 451421 (trade)
Web: www.customandcommercial.com

Euro Car Parts
Euro House
Fulton Road
Wembley
Middlesex HA9 0TF
England
Tel: 020 8956 5050
Web: www.europarts.com; branches throughout UK
Parts.

Gary Wilkie
c/o Stroud Engineering & Welding
200 Westward Road
Stroud

Gloucester GL5 4ST
England
Tel: 01453 750960/822522
Restoration.

Henley Beetles Ltd
Unit 8
Northfield Avenue
Henley on Thames, RG9 3PA
England
Tel 0118 940 3464
Restoration.

Herinckx Coachworks
229-235 Fairfax Drive
Westcliffe on Sea
Essex SS90 9EP.
England
Tel: 01702 339979
Restoration and repairs.

Just Aircooled
43 Hermitage Road
Bridlington
East Yorks, YO16 4HF
Tel: 01262 671962
Web: www.justaircooled.co.uk

John Forbes Automotive
7 Meadow Lane
Edinburgh EH8 9NR
Scotland.
Tel: 0774 260964
Web: http://forbesautomotive.co.uk/index.htm
Sales, service, repairs & parts.

Just Kampers
Unit 1 Stapeley Manor
Long Lane
Odiham
Hants, RG29 1JE
Tel: 01256 862288
Web: www.justkampers.com

Karmann Ghia Centre
Tel: 01442 833209
Web: www.kgcentre.co.uk
Email: kgcentre@dircon.co.uk

Karmann Konnection
289 Victoria Avenue
Southend-on-Sea, SS2 6NE
Tel: 01702 340613
Fax: 01702 332718
Web: karmannkonnection.com
Repairs, service & parts.

Kingfisher Kustoms
Unit 5 Oldbury Road
Smethwick
Warley
West Midlands B66 1NU
England
Tel: 0121 558 9135
Fax: 0121 558 9791
Parts.

Machine 7 Air-cooled Parts
Unit 2 Liberty Way
Attleborough Fields Industrial Estate
Nuneaton
Warickshire, CV11 6RZ
Web: www.machine7.com

Martin McGarry
Motorworks
Mansfield, NG19 0HW
Notts
England
Tel: 01623 656443 (tel/fax)
Web: www.karmannghia motorworks.co.uk
Email: info@karmann-ghia.co.uk
Imports and restoration. New & used KG parts.

Martin Murray
Clonbrick
Monard
Tipperary
Ireland
Tel: 353 62 76177
Parts.

Megabug
Unit 3 Whiteheart Road
Plumstead
London SE18 1DG
England
Tel: 020 8317 7333
Fax: 020 8855 4289
Web: www.megabug.co.uk
Email: info@megabug.co.uk
Parts.

Nasbugs Ltd.
Unit 18-2, Seven Sisters
Tottenham
London, N15 4QF
England
Tel: 020 8808 2228
Fax: 020 8808 8889
Restoration, servicing & parts.

Spirit of the 50s
Reindeer Park
Kingsbury Road
Sutton Coldfield, B76 0DE
Tel: 01675 479775
Web: www.spiritofthe50s.co.uk

Stevens VW Dismantlers
Drakes Lane Industrial Estate
Boreham
Chelmsford
Essex, CM3 3BE
Tel: 01245 362020
Parts.

Vee Wee VW Parts
Tel: 0121 749 8832
Web: www.veewee.com

Volksbits
56 Bristol Road
Gloucester GL1 5SD
England
Tel: 01452 414665.
Tel: 087 05143 397 (mail order hotline)

Volksbits
800 Pershore Road
Selly Park
Birmingham, B45 5EW
Tel:0905 1010739
Web: www.volksbits.co.uk

Volkscraft Classics
Drakes Holdings
Ferry Road
Fiskerton
Lincoln
England
Tel: 01522 595407
Repairs, parts & servicing.

Volksmagic
111a Park Lane
Tel: 0121 541 22778
Web: www.volksmagic.com
Parts & repairs.

Volkspares
104-106 Newlands Park
Sydenham
London, SE26 5N3
Tel: 020 8778 0710
Web: www.volkspares.co.uk

Volkspares
591 High Road
Leytonstone
London, E11 4PA
Tel 020 8539 0513
Web: www.volkspares.co.uk

VW Books
28 Longnor Road
Telford, TF1 3NY
Web: www.vwbooks.co.uk
Email: sales@vwbooks.co.uk
Books and publications (inc. mail order) on all Volkswagen subjects.

VW Heritage
47 Dolphin Road
Shoreham by Sea
West Sussex, BN43 6PB
Tel: 01273 444000
Web: www.vwheritage.com

VW Speedshop
47B Kingshill Road
Chorlton
Manchester M21 9HD
England
Tel/Fax: 0161 881 5999
Parts.

VW Speedshop
Unit 12
Ackworth Road Industrial Estate
Hilsea
Portsmouth
Hants PO3 6RY
Tel: 01283 812019
Web: www.speedshop.com
Parts.

Westside Motors
R/O 34/36 The Broadway
Woodford Green
Essex IG8 0HQ
England
Tel: 020 8505 5215
Tel: 0831 580316 (mobile).
Restoration parts.

Wizard Roadsters
497 Ipswich Road
Trading Estate
Slough
Berkshire SL1 4EP
England
Tel: 01753 551555
Fax: 01753 550770
Web: www.wizardroadsters.com
Conversion specialists.

Clubs
AUSTRIA
Karmann Ghia Club Austria
www.karmannghia.at

AUSTRALIA
Australian VW Car Clubs
www.volksculture.com

Club VeeDub
www.clubvw.org.au

Australian Volkswagen Clubs & Associations
www.ozvolks.com
Karmann Ghia Owners Club Australia
karmannghiaownersclubaustralia.com

Karmann Ghia owners Club of Victoria
www.shannons.co.au
Volks Enthusiasts Club of South Australia
www.volksenthusiasts.org.au

BELGIUM
Karmann Ghia Club of Belgium
Postiljonstraat 14
1180 Brussel

Kever & Karmann Ghia Cabrio Club Belgie
www.kevercabrioletclub.be

BRAZIL
Fusca Clube Do Brazil
Caixa Postal 60131
cep 05096-970 Sau Paulo/SP
Brazil
Tel: 55 11 2207071
Fax: 55 11 220 7771

Karmann Ghia Club Rio de Janeiro
Tel (5521) 359-4800 or 359-4855

KG Clube de Belo Horizonte
Email: kgcbh@terr.co.br

BRITAIN
Association of British VW Owners' Clubs
www.abvwc.com

Historic Volkswagen Club
www.historicvws.co.uk

Karmann Ghia Owners' Club
www.kgoc-gb.org

Split Screen Van Club (for pre-1968 VW Type 2)
Steve Childs
96 Western Road
Silver End
Witham
Essex CM8 3SG
England
Tel: 01376 84397

Volkswagen Owners' Club (GB)
www.vwocgb.com

VW Club UK
www.classicvolks.com

VW Type 3 & 4 Club
www.vwtype3and4club.org.uk

Wizard Owners' Club
Glynn Harper
24 Laurel Avenue Kendray
Barnsley
Yorkshire ST0 3JA
England

DENMARK
Dansk Karmann Ghia Klub
www.karmannghia.dk

FRANCE
Karmann Ghia – Les Club –
Karmann-Ghia Volkswagen
www.karman-ghia.org

Karmann-Ghia Club de France
Fourets.alain@wanadoo.fr

Karmann Ghia Owners Club France
Karmann-ghia.org

Vintage VW Club de France,
Karmann Ghia section
www.vintagevw.org

GERMANY
IG der Karmann Ghia
Fahrer-/innen, Uwe Witkowski,
Kratzenburger Str.7, 56283 Ney/
Hensrück

Karmann Ghia IG Südheide
Tel: 05145/93052

Karmann Ghia Club Karlsruhe e. V.
Tel: 0721/784187

Karmann Ghia Club Kassel e.V
Tel: 05542/1084

Karmann Ghia Club Südhessen im KGVD
Tel: 06023-2231, email:
101.133924@germ,anynet.de

Karmann Ghia Freunde Nordbayern
Tel: 09805/7904

Karmann Ghia IG Bochum
Rolf Siegner, Karl Leichstr.11, 44805 Bochum

Karmann Ghia IG Köln,
Ingo Graf, Siegurger Str.153, 50679 Köln

Karmann Ghia IG Kreis Pinnebeg,
Peer Schmidt-Ohm, VoBstraat 23, 22399 Hamburg

Karmann Ghia IG Wesel

Tel: 0281/50833

INDIA
BPPT VE Owners' Club
Drs Agus Pramudya
JL MH Tharmira No 8
Ged BPPT Lt 7
Dikiat Jakarta
Pusat
India.

ITALY
Karmann Ghia Club Italia
https://thesportscoupe.com; www.karmannghia.it

Maggiolino Club Italy
PO Box 11027
Saint Vincente
Italy.
Tel: 39 48 0931

NETHERLANDS
The Karmann Ghia Club of the Netherlands
www.karmannghiaclub.nl

Keverclub Nederland
Gerard Wilkie
Postbus 7538 5601jm
Eindhoven
Netherlands.

Luchtgekoelde VW Club Nederland
Van Geerstraat 7
2351 PL Leiderdorp
Netherlands.

NEW ZEALAND
Kombined VW Club
www.kombinedclub.org.nz
Canterbury Volkswagen Enthusiast Club, New Zealand
www.canterburyclub.co.nz

Volkswagen Owners Club – Auckland
www.vwownersclub.co.nz

PORTUGAL
Club VW Air Clube de Portugal
www.bugbus.net

SOUTH AFRICA
Beetle & Karmann Ghia Club – Aircooled South Africa
www.aircooledvwsa.co.za

The Volkswagen Club of South Africa
www.vwclub.co.za

SPAIN
Club Clasicos Volkswagen De Alicante
PO Box 420
E 03080 Alicante
Spain.
Tel: 34 65 20 0777

SWEDEN
Air-coolers Vasteras
PO Box 3070
S-720 03 Vasteras
Sweden.

Bugrunners
Lena Lilliehorn
Box 1141 Jarnvagsgatan 8
S-581 11 Linkoping
Sweden.

SWITZERLAND
Der Club – Karmann-Ghia Schweiz
www.karmann-ghia.ch

USA
56-59 Karmann Ghia Registry
Jeffrey P Lipnichan
961 Village Road
Lancaster
PA 17602
USA.
Tel: 717 464 0969

The Karmann Ghia Club of North America
www.karmannghia.org

Vintage Volkswagen Club of America
817 5th Street
Cresson
PA 16630
USA.

For further information visit the internet or consult the following websites regarding international clubs:

Karmann Ghia Connection www.karmannghiaconnection.com
Classic Volks wwwclassicvolks.com

Bibliography

Karmann Ghia Coupé & Convertible • Malcolm Bobbitt • Veloce Publishing Ltd
Volkswagen Beetle Colour Family Album • Sparrow • Veloce Publishing Ltd
Volkswagen Beetle: The Car of the 20th Century • Richard Copping • Veloce Publishing Ltd
VW Beetle Cabriolet • Malcolm Bobbitt • Veloce Publishing Ltd
VW Custom Beetle Colour Family Album • Sparrow • Veloce Publishing Ltd
Small Wonder • Walter Henry Nelson • Hutchinson
Volkswagen Beetle • Marco Batazzi • Giorgio Nada Editore
VW Treasures by Karmann • Jan P Norbye • Motorbooks
The VW Beetle including Karmann Ghia • Jonathan Wood • Motor Racing Publications
Essential Volkswagen Karmann Ghia • Laurence Meredith • Bay View Books
Original VW Beetle • Laurence Meredith • Bay View Books
VW Beetle Convertible 1949-80 • Walter Zeichner • Schiffer Publishing Co.
Illustrated Volkswagen Buyers' Guide • Peter Vack • Motorbooks
Karmann Ghia 1955-82 • Brooklands Books
Advertising the Beetle • Compiled by Daniel Young • Yesteryear Books
Volkswagen Beetle Coachbuilts and Cabriolets 1940-60 • Keith Seume and Bob Shail • Bay View Books
Beetle: Chronicles of the People's Car volumes 1-3 • Etzold • G T Foulis
Volkswagen Beetle • Bill Boddy • Osprey

Motor magazine
Autocar magazine
Practical Classics Magazine
VW Motoring magazine
Volksworld magazine
Classic VWs magazine

INDEX

Alfa Romeo 6
Austin 6
Austin-Healey 22, 28, 43

Beeskow, Johannes 38
BMW 6, 22
Boano, Gian 8
Boano, Mario 8, 9
Boehner, Ludwig 7
Borgward 22

Chevrolet 26
Chrysler 8-10
Citroën 36, 42
Coggiola, Sergio 8

DKW 7, 21

Exner, Virgil 9-10

Feuereissen, Dr K 7, 9, 11, 17, 21
Fiat 6, 12, 26, 38
Ford 7

Ghia 6, 8-11, 15-17, 27, 34, 36, 38, 40, 43
Goggomobil 38

Hebmüller 12
Hino 22

Karmann 6, 10-12, 16, 27, 28, 38, 40
Karmann, Wilhelm 6-8, 16, 21, 22-23
Karmann, Wilhelm (Jr) 7-8, 16, 22, 38

Keller, K.T 9
King, Henry 9

Ladouche, Charles 8, 9, 11, 21
Lincoln 38
Lloyd 38
Loewy, Raymond 9

MG 22, 43

Nordhoff, Heinz 7, 9, 11, 17, 21, 38-40
NSU 38

Plymouth 9
Porsche 92
Porsche, Ferdinand 92

Renault 6, 22, 43
Reuters, Ernst 67
Rometsch 38

Sartorelli, Sergio 36, 38
Segre, Luigi 7-11, 17, 21, 22, 36
Simca 22
Skoda 22
Société France Motors 9
Studebaker 9
Sunbeam 22

Thomas, C.B 9
Tjaarda, Tom 36-38
Tracta 12
Triumph 22

Volkswagen:
    Brazil factory 30, 48-49
    Golf 48

111

K70 48
  Schimmwagen 15
  Scirocco 48
  Type 2 15, 34
  Type 3 34, 36, 38-40, 43
  Type 147 34

Volvo 6, 22

Westfalia 34